PUB WALKS

—— IN ——

South London

Leigh Hatts

D1634844

COUNTRYSIDE BOOKS

NEWBURY, BERKSHIRE

First published 2001
© Leigh Hatts 2001

All rights reserved. No reproduction
permitted without the prior permission
of the publisher:

COUNTRYSIDE BOOKS
3 Catherine Road
Newbury, Berkshire

ISBN 1 85306 659 1

Designed by Graham Whiteman
Photographs by the author
Maps by Gelder design and mapping

Produced through MRM Associates Ltd., Reading
Typeset by Techniset Typesetters, Newton-le-Willows
Printed by J. W. Arrowsmith Ltd., Bristol

Contents

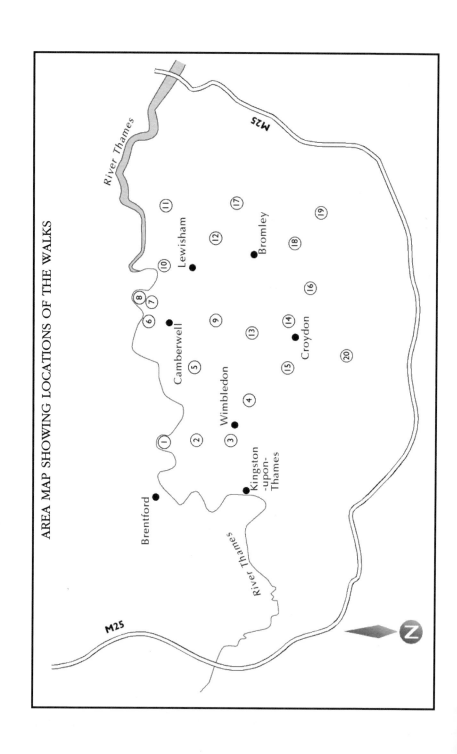

AREA MAP SHOWING LOCATIONS OF THE WALKS

Walk

PUBLISHER'S NOTE

We hope that you obtain considerable enjoyment from this book; great care has been taken in its preparation. However, changes of landlord and actual closures are sadly not uncommon. Likewise, although at the time of publication all routes followed public rights of way or permitted paths, diversion orders can be made and permissions withdrawn.

We cannot of course be held responsible for such diversion orders and any inaccuracies in the text which result from these or any other changes to the routes nor any damage which might result from walkers trespassing on private property. We are anxious though that all details covering the walks and the pubs are kept up to date and would therefore welcome information from readers which would be relevant to future editions.

INTRODUCTION

Most London pub guides still concentrate on London north of the River Thames although to the south there are many unspoilt gems. Some of the oldest inns are to be found in Southwark which, if you draw a line on the map, is further north than Buckingham Palace.

But if the Thames is still a barrier it is a wonderful backdrop to such ancient pubs as the Angel on Bermondsey Wall. The George, the National Trust's pub, owes its origin to London Bridge closing its gate at night and creating a demand for overnight accommodation in what was then 'Surrey' opposite the City. To the west at Barnes the curving Thames creates a virtual island with the Sun Inn presiding in the middle of its village.

Further away in deeper South London there are some little known pockets of countryside which help to preserve the concept of London being a string of villages and throw a green belt around such bursting conurbations as Croydon and Bromley. These walks occasionally coincide with paths, co-ordinated by the London Walking Forum, making up the new 150 mile London Outer Orbital Path, known as the London Loop, which circles the capital using 24 sections. Some of the best countryside has survived due to the National Trust, as at Chislehurst, and the Corporation of London, as at Old Coulsdon. Thanks to such countryside management the paths tend to be in good order. Indeed the urban fringe countryside has just been expanded both alongside Mitcham Common and at Norwood to create 'new' countryside on land once reserved for waterworks and sewage. And the increased access to areas such as these has resulted in several pubs being reborn to cater for those discovering new places to enjoy their leisure time.

Young's, now with many pubs in South London, has been brewing on the banks of the River Wandle for over 150 years and two walks feature attractive places in its green corridor. The Wandle was a trout stream as recently as the 1850s and winds north from Croydon. Recurring landmarks on the walks include Canary Wharf which can be seen on half a dozen of the routes. A new landmark is the Wheel on the South Bank. All landmarks from south to north are visible in good weather on the walk from Mottingham.

The standard of drink, food and welcome in London's pubs continues to rise, with food having now become as important as drink. This is partly due to public demand and the result of young chefs finding that by working for a pub, or even owning one, they have the opportunities not immediately available in restaurants. Certainly many like to be able to have instant reaction from customers who would not bother with a more formal dining establishment.

The all day opening of pubs, at first only welcomed by some in the licensed trade and opposed by those fearing an increase in city centre drunkenness, is proving a quiet success. Pubs are returning to being 'inns' in the old tradition — open all day, serving not just alcohol but coffee and tea, providing good value food and welcoming children. Some are even going back to offering bed and breakfast.

If you are leaving your car in a pub car park whilst going on the walk it is advisable to check first with the staff although normally there will not be any problems (assuming that you are a patron, of course). But whilst there is much countryside locked into South London it is advisable not to assume that car travel is always best. In 'south central' London, such as Southwark, public transport is always best since some pubs cannot offer parking and street parking is almost non-existent. But South London probably has even better public transport than North London.

One most exciting development in South London is the introduction in Millennium Year 2000 of the Tramlink system linking Wimbledon with Norwood. A decade ago it was only at Fleetwood in Lancashire that you could ride down a high street in a tram. Today in Croydon you travel not only within feet of shops but past a Tudor almshouse. Later the tram is speeding through National Trust parkland. The best way to arrive at Addington Village Inn is by tram to enjoy the ride through the woods and the fast run down Gravel Hill. It is also the best way home after the walk and refreshment in the very family-friendly pub. The one day Travelcard allows unlimited travel on buses, trains, tubes and trams.

Each walk is circular and the accompanying sketch maps are intended to give a simple guide to the route. Details of the relevant Ordnance Survey Explorer (1:25 000) maps for each area are also given. Alternatively, you might find a London street atlas useful for many of the routes.

These are easy walks and with all day opening at most pubs you can have a drink at the start and the end. Neither walking nor refreshment should be hurried.

Leigh Hatts

1 Barnes
The Sun Inn

Barnes is a village on a peninsula protected by the River Thames on three sides and its pond and common on the fourth. The many enforced closures of ancient Hammersmith Bridge only serve to enhance the rural remoteness here. The walk passes alongside Europe's largest urban wetland centre and includes a stretch on the Thames towpath, following part of the course of the annual Oxford and Cambridge Boat Race.

The Sun is an 18th-century coaching inn opposite the pond with plenty of ducks. Round the back of the inn is Barnes Bowling Club where Elizabeth I is said to have been taught to play by Sir Francis Drake and local resident Sir Francis Walsingham. Also by the pond is Milbourne House where novelist Henry Fielding lived.

The view can be enjoyed from the tables outside and by the pond but the inside is also a delight with its jumble of dark rooms and corners filled with old furniture. The walls feature former local views, including the church before its rebuilding and cricket pictures. There is a central bar but this pub cannot be described as open plan.

Food is a big attraction here with soup, sandwiches, jacket potatoes, salads and at least three vegetarian dishes always available. Puddings include apple pie. This is a Allied Domecq house with six Tetley's ales and a changing selection of guest ales along with Fuller's London Pride from Chiswick, just across the river. It is open all day and food is served at lunchtime. Telephone: 020 8876 5256.

- **HOW TO GET THERE:** The Sun is in Church Road SW13 opposite Barnes Pond. Buses 9, 9A and R61 stop almost outside. There is a pleasant walk from Barnes Station — turn left from the station house and just before reaching houses go half-right on a narrow metalled path. Cross a road and keep ahead to Barnes Pond.
- **PARKING:** There is a car park at the pub for patrons.
- **LENGTH OF THE WALK:** 3¹/₂ miles. Map: OS Explorer 161 London South (GR 219764).

THE WALK

1. Turn left from the pub gateway to walk along Church Road. Beyond the shops is the church which was consecrated in 1215 by Archbishop Langton on his way back from Runnymede where he had secured the agreement of King John to Magna Carta. The church is a surprise for although the exterior appears ancient much of the inside and north side have been rebuilt in modern style following a fire in 1978. However, the 16th-century tower survived with the clock in working order. Continue to the crossroads.

2. Go ahead past the Red Lion and down Queen Elizabeth Walk which is named after Elizabeth I who in the 1580s came here three times to visit statesman Sir Frances Walsingham whose mansion stood to the right. Whilst living here Sir Francis secured the conviction and execution of Mary Queen of Scots. On the left is the Barnes Wetland Centre (see below), opened by the Wildfowl and Wetlands Trust in 2000. This, Europe's largest urban wetland project, has been created on 105 acres of redundant reservoirs. The lagoons, ponds, reed beds and seasonally flooded wetlands are designed to attract the birds which migrate along the River Thames every year. The way narrows to run ahead to the Thames towpath.

3. Turn left upstream. Soon there is the University Boat Race mile post. Later there is Harrods Villge, a recent development around Harrods landmark 1893 furniture depository once used for the storage of furniture and possessions by those taking up postings in the Empire.

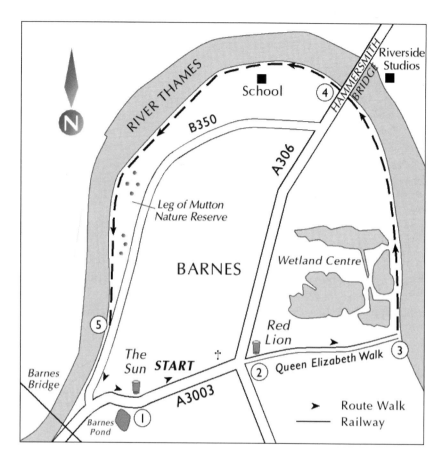

Other buildings here include a converted soap factory and a candle factory. Opposite, just before the Riverside Studios, is the site of Brandenburgh House. This was Queen Caroline's house which can be seen in a picture on the wall of the Princess of Wales pub at Blackheath (Walk 10).

4. Pass under Hammersmith Bridge which dates back to the 1820s. The original suspension bridge was built by William Tierney Clark who was responsible for linking Buda and Pest with a crossing. The first Hammersmith Bridge is seen in Walter Greaves' painting *Hammersmith Bridge on Boat Race Day*. The towpath bends south past St Paul's School grounds. Soon there is Chiswick across the water with Fuller's brewery rising above the houses. Hops and malt used to arrive by barge. Until 1934 there was a ferry from the towpath to Chiswick church. Artist William Hogarth is buried in the churchyard — hence the Hogarth Roundabout which divides the village. Residential Church Wharf, upstream of the church, was once occupied by Thornycroft shipbuilding which moved to Southampton in 1904 when destroyers became too large to pass under the Thames bridges. Corney Reach Pier, also opposite, is on the site of Corney House visited by Elizabeth I in 1602. Leg O'Mutton nature reserve, by the towpath, is another former reservoir.

5. On reaching Barnes continue along the waterfront towards Barnes Bridge. The footbridge, attached in 1895, was built strong enough to hold a capacity Boat Race crowd. But before the bridge go left up the High Street to the pond and the Sun Inn.

ATTRACTION ON THE ROUTE
Barnes Wetland Centre is in Queen Elizabeth Walk SW13. It was the vision of Sir Peter Scott, founder of the Wildfowl and Wetlands Trust at Slimbridge on the River Severn, that a wetland centre should be developed in London. Work began in 1995 and the unveiling of a bronze statue of Peter Scott marked the official opening in 2000. The Peter Scott Visitor Centre includes a glass observatory, an art gallery, lecture theatre, café and shop. Live pictures of wildfowl are relayed by CCTV to the centre. Open 9.30 am to 6 pm (winter 5 pm) every day except 25 December. Admission charge. Telephone: 020 8409 4400.

2 Putney Heath
The Green Man

Putney Heath is the woodland, rather than heathland, on the hill above Putney which was still a village well into the 19th century. People started living around the heath in the 13th century and by the 16th century Roehampton on the south side had become fashionable. The main road up from Putney has always been important as it linked to the Putney-Fulham ferry and, from 1729, the bridge. In 1812 John Constable breakfasted at Putney before coming up the hill to sketch at Putney Heath. Today the walker will still experience countryside only a short distance from now busy Putney.

The name Green Man is common even in London. The figure is found carved in churches and in London on May Day a green man dressed in leaves would lead dancing in the streets to welcome spring. The name is also associated with Robin Hood and even here on Putney Heath there have been suggestions about such a connection. This Green Man pub is two early 18th-century back to back cottages and has been likened to the Bull in *The Archers*. Claims that it stands on the site of a

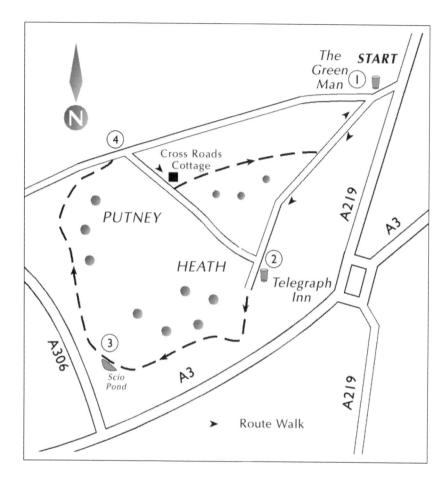

smithy run by the father of Thomas Cromwell, Henry VIII's henchman, are hard to prove. But numerous legends continue to be associated with the inn. Dick Turpin is said to have hidden his pistols here and another highwayman was allegedly hanged outside. Certainly footpads robbed people leaving here late at night. Today the view is of the number 14 bus terminus by a cattle pound.

At the end of the 19th century poet Algernon Swinburn, who lived at the bottom of Putney Hill in a house now marked by a blue plaque, often called in here on his daily walk to the Rose & Crown in Wimbledon.

There are two small cosy bars with shove ha'penny and the now very rare ring the bull games, still played here as well as darts. Outside there are two patios and a surprise garden with a children's play area.

Putney Heath

The food is home cooked and varies according to the season and weather. You will always find soup and sandwiches and the hot dishes include a vegetarian dish. This is a Young's house with Young's beers and Guinness available. It is open from 12 noon to 2.30 pm all year with evening opening as well during the summer months. Telephone: 020 8788 8096.

- **HOW TO GET THERE:** The Green Man is in Wildcroft Road on the edge of Putney Heath and at the top of Putney Hill. Bus 14 runs from Putney Station up the hill to turn round outside the pub.
- **PARKING:** There is street parking further along Wildcroft Road.
- **LENGTH OF THE WALK:** 2 miles. Map: OS Explorer 161 London South (GR 237743).

THE WALK

1. Turn right out of the pub. Cross the junction and continue along Wildcroft Road. After the cattle pound (left) there is woodland on both sides. At the end, beyond a fenced reservoir, is the Telegraph pub. The name comes from the Admiralty telegraph, a large frame with shutters, which stood nearby on this high ground passing messages from Portsmouth to Whitehall. Constable paused to sketch the structure.

2. Continue ahead to the end of the road by the entrance to Wildcroft

Manor. Here take the right fork to follow the woodland path near flats. After the path turns sharply right keep ahead on the left fork. The path runs gently downhill. Soon there are houses over to the right. Keep forward to Scio Pond, named after a now demolished house nearby which a Greek resident in the 19th century named after the island of his birth. Walk along the right hand side of the pond to meet a firm path at a T-junction.

3. Turn right and at once take the left fork. Later in the open another path joins from the right. Soon over to the left is a view of Holy Trinity, Roehampton's 200 foot spire completed in 1898. Just past the war memorial (right) and before the road ahead, go right on a gravel path. This runs parallel to the road (left) and eventually joins it.

4. Keep ahead to turn right into Telegraph Road passing a 'beware deer' sign. Follow the pavement as far as Cross Roads Cottage on the left. Here go through the gateway on the left side of the cottage. At the back bear right. Continue to follow this path and ignore all turnings. There is a glimpse of a cricket field to the right on the way. The path runs through woodland to Wildcroft Road. Turn left for the Green Man.

③ Crooked Billet, Woodhayes Road
The Hand in Hand

Wimbledon Common provides endless opportunities for visiting pubs and taking long walks over open land and in woodland. There are over a thousand acres of real managed countryside with sometimes muddy paths and rangers on horseback. Surprises include a windmill, a hidden pond, a small Thames tributary and a literary association. Such is the network of paths that this walk can either be a long circular trip or a short walk to visit the windmill. Those completing the full circuit will find the all day opening at the Hand in Hand handy.

The Hand in Hand is in a charming corner of Wimbledon known as the Crooked Billet. A few yards away is another pub called the Crooked Billet which has a 16th-century barn behind. In summer drinkers from both pubs mingle on the grass outside. Both are Young's pubs so it does not matter greatly if glasses are returned to the wrong building. The name Hand in Hand sometimes means 'hand and heart' suggesting a friendly greeting. Here the hint on the sign is of lovers' hands and this is certainly a romantic spot.

This award-winning pub is made up of four low-ceilinged 18th and 19th-century cottages joined together. Once it was a bakehouse which started selling beer and it remained an alehouse until as late as 1974 when Young's took over. There is a central bar and a children's room near the main entrance. In winter a log fire usually burns in the bar area making the interior cosy. In summer the cramped entrance yard, shaded by a tree, is decorated with flower baskets and window boxes.

The menu includes dishes such as shepherd's pie, popular home-made pasta and cod in Young's beer batter with chips. There are also always burgers, salads and vegetarian lasagne. Young's beers are available along with Beamish stout, guest beers and a wide selection of wines. Open all day. Telephone: 020 8946 5720.

- **HOW TO GET THERE:** The Hand in Hand is at Crooked Billet on the edge of Wimbledon Common off Woodhayes Road SW19. Bus 200 runs from Wimbledon Station to the end of Woodhayes Road.
- **PARKING:** There is street parking nearby.
- **LENGTH OF THE WALK:** 5 miles. Map: OS Explorer 161 London South (GR 234707).

THE WALK

1. Turn left out of the pub and go left again up West Side Common. Among the houses facing the common are Westside House, home of the Lord Chancellor Lord Lyndhurst in the 1820s and later Spencer Gore, the 1877 and first Wimbledon Tennis Champion, lived here. Soon there is Cannizaro House, named after the Duke of Cannizaro who lived here in the early 19th century. Continue to the far end but do not turn left with the road.

2. Instead take the left fork ahead across the Common. This path soon meets a wide firm path. Here turn right and follow this path all the way to the windmill. On reaching the cluster of houses around the mill continue forward to walk anti-clockwise round the circle to find the windmill entrance.

Wimbledon's windmill, built in 1817, is the only remaining example of a hollow-post flour mill (see below for opening times). After the 1860s it was used as just a residence. Lord Baden-Powell wrote *Scouting for Boys* here five years before the first Scout Camp in 1907.

3. A short diversion would take you east along Windmill Road to the main road where, by the bus stop, there is the Apostolic Nunciature — the Vatican Embassy. This is where Pope John Paul stayed during his

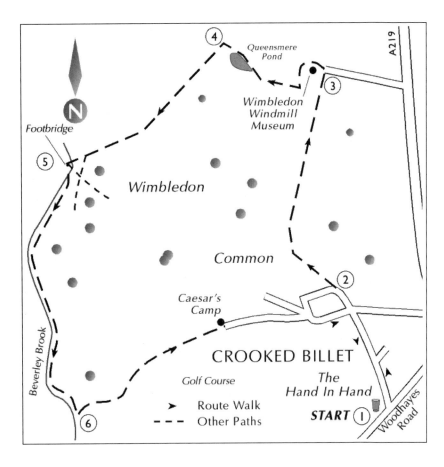

visit to Britain in 1981. It was also here that His Holiness's now familiar coat of arms was designed because at the time of his election the Vatican envoy here was also the Holy See's heraldry expert.

The main walk continues past the windmill entrance and round the corner to pass the tearoom and the London & Scottish Golf Club. Turn left and continue on the narrow path running to the right. At the corner of the buildings go right down a long straight path running through the wood. The path is downhill with sometimes water running on both sides. At the bottom is Queensmere Pond which was dug in 1887 to mark Queen Victoria's Golden Jubilee. Keep to the right of the pond and at the far end continue ahead through the trees.

4. At a T-junction go left to follow Stag Ride on the wooded edge of the Common. Through the trees to the right there is a glimpse of Putney

Vale Cemetery. Continue, ignoring all turnings. Later there is a view (right) of a war memorial. Where the path runs out into the open at a triangle of grass go right. Just after the paths meet the way is between a playing field and the Beverley Brook (left). At once turn sharp left to follow the water upstream.

5. With the water to the right stay on the woodland riverside path. The Beverley Brook rises in Richmond Park and runs into the Thames opposite Fulham Football Club. A stone marks the boundary between Wandsworth and Merton ahead. Across the water is the Royal Borough of Kingston. Pass a brick bridge carrying Robin Hood Ride. Continue south and after a bend at Mill Corner the riverside path ends by a bridge. Turn sharp left at this junction.

6. The path runs through trees and is briefly fenced at Beverley Meads Nature Reserve. The path climbs gently to cross a fenced path leading to Warren Farm. The way ahead is now also fenced as it continues to climb gently across the Royal Wimbledon Golf Course. Just before the trees ahead the path passes through an Iron Age fort known as Caesar's Camp — the mown banks can be seen each side of the path. At the far end the path meets a road at a bend. Go ahead along Camp Road, with buildings to the right, to reach the golf club house at a junction. Ahead is the former William Wilberforce School, an octagonal 1760's building for fifty poor children. Bear right to pass Camp Farm. The road has a high brick wall on the right and almshouses and the Fox and Grapes on the left. At the end go right to walk back down West Side Common. At the far end go right for the Hand in Hand.

ATTRACTION ON THE ROUTE
Wimbledon Windmill now has a museum on the first floor. Open weekends April to October 2 pm to 5 pm. Admission charge. Telephone: 020 8947 2825.

Merton Abbey Mills SW19
The William Morris

The River Wandle rises in Croydon and flows out into the Thames at Wandsworth. One of the most important buildings on this river was Merton Priory where, just over 300 years after Henry VIII closed the monastery, Arthur Liberty of Liberty's Regent Street store and William Morris set up dyeing and block printing works. The water was thought to have a special quality for dyeing. Morris was downstream and Liberty said: 'We sent our dirty water down to Morris.' The walk embraces a farm and National Trust parkland as well as a stretch of the river.

William Morris (1834–1896) was an early socialist, writer, artist and manufacturer. The William Morris pub only opened in 1990 but it is at least 90 years old having been built by Arthur Liberty of Liberty's store as the Block Shop for storing Morris's printing blocks. The building is just one of a group which make up Merton Abbey Mills, the former Liberty Print Works, which has become a popular craft centre. The wheelhouse, or mill, which is the logo for the London Borough of Merton, is here. The Colour House is much older than the pub having been built in 1730 incorporating material from Merton Priory (it was never an abbey) which stood on the site. The main monastic buildings were to the east and are now cut through by Merantun Way. Here St Thomas Becket was educated, Henry I's body lay in state, Queen Eleanor of Provence was crowned and her husband Henry III held a peace conference with the Dauphin.

The pub has seating overlooking the river and framed Morris prints on the walls. Outdoor seating is popular in the summer. Lunchtime food includes sandwiches and jacket potatoes. There is also food available in the evening. This is a freehouse and so there are always guest beers. The pub is open all day but is busy at weekends when the Merton Abbey Mills Market is open. Telephone: 020 8540 0216.

- **HOW TO GET THERE:** The William Morris is at Merton Abbey Mills in Watermill Way off the A24 Merantun Way just south of Colliers Wood. The nearest Underground station is Colliers Wood (Northern Line). Approaching on foot, turn left from the station and having crossed Merton Bridge follow the Wandle which leaves High Street by the Savacentre. Continue by the water to a bridge. Cross the road to find an archway almost opposite. Cross Merantun Way and go ahead with the river. Turn left to enter Merton Abbey Mills and find the William Morris.
- **PARKING:** There is car park at Merton Abbey Mills.
- **LENGTH OF THE WALK:** 2¹/₂ miles. Map: OS Explorer 161 London South (GR 265698).

THE WALK

1. From the pub front door go ahead and turn left to pass between the Merton Abbey Mills buildings. Beyond the mill (left) go left to cross the River Wandle. Turn left to walk upstream with the water on the left. Across the Wandle is the William Morris. The path runs through trees to Windsor Avenue. Beyond here the way ahead is wide and metalled as this is also the approach to Deen City Farm. At the junction by Phipps Bridge, where a mill was recorded in 1263, the right turn is for the farm where there are horses, cows, sheep, goats, chickens, ducks and an owl. Visitors are welcome in the daytime.

2. At the junction go ahead into the grounds of Morden Hall Park which is now in the care of the National Trust. A straight path runs across Bunce's Meadow which is named after a late-19th-century farmer. At the far end the way bends to a junction by a stream. The way

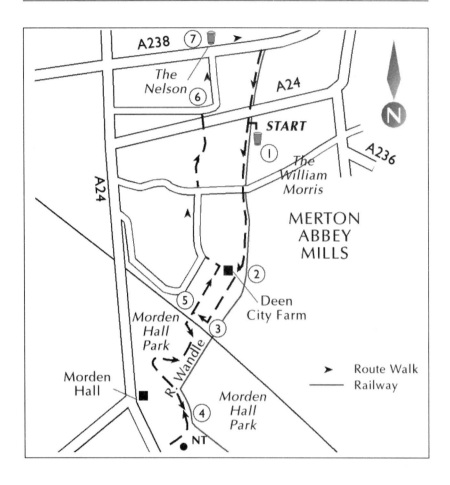

back is to the right but to visit the National Trust complex in the estate buildings of Morden Hall turn left and go over the Tramway level crossing.

3. The path is fenced after the tram line. At the junction go left to follow a winding path across the marshland and meadows in the park, coloured white and yellow by wild flowers in summer. Beyond a bridge go left and over two more bridges spanning watercourses. Morden Hall, built about 1750 and now a restaurant, is over to the right.

4. Just before the white iron bridge go right towards the buildings to find Morden Cottage and the snuff mill. The stables, National Trust shop and café can be visited. To return to the William Morris retrace the path to the Tramway level crossing.

5. Beyond the level crossing go ahead on a path by a stream. There are printworks to the right. At the far end go up steps to a metalled path. Turn left to reach Deer Park Road. Go right to pass the Sunlight Laundry. At the T-junction with Jubilee Way go ahead in front of the Shendale building to find a sunken footpath running north. At the far end use the crossing to go over Merantun Way.

6. Merantun Way was a railway line and the crossing here was a level crossing for this footpath. Go ahead into High Path. Turn right and left up Abbey Road to pass Station Road (right). At the far end there is the Nelson with a large glazed picture of HMS *Victory*. This stands on the site of the entrance to Merton Place, home of Lady Hamilton. Admiral Lord Nelson spent much time at the house and here the couple had their last meeting before the fatal Battle of Trafalgar.

7. Go right along Merton High Street until the River Wandle appears on the right by the Savacentre hypermarket. Do not cross the river but go sharp right on the riverside path. Almost at once there is a plaque (left, by the water) recording the position of the Morris works. Continue ahead to the bridge. Cross the road to find an archway almost opposite. Cross Merantun Way and go ahead with the river. Turn left to enter Merton Mills and return to the William Morris.

ATTRACTIONS ON THE ROUTE

Merton Abbey Mills Market, which includes food and craft stalls, operates every Saturday and Sunday from 10 am to 5 pm. Telephone: 020 8543 9608. *Morden Hall Park* was the parkland of a private residence until 1941 when it passed to the National Trust. Cows grazed here as late as the 1970s. A riverside shop and café open daily (except 25 and 26 December and 1 January) from 10 am to 5 pm. Telephone: 020 8687 0881.

⑤ Clapham Common
The Windmill on the Common

*Clapham Common was drained in 1722 and in 1816 roaming pigs were
finally banished. The 220 acres have been gradually surrounded by houses
since the 18th century but no new building has encroached apart from
handsome Holy Trinity church in the corner. Those who have lived here
include William Wilberforce, Captain Cook, historian Lord Macaulay and
architects Charles Barry (Houses of Parliament) and John Francis Bentley
(Westminster Cathedral). This walks links the Commons of Clapham and
Wandsworth by way of the Falcon Brook valley.*

The Windmill pub has existed since at least 1665 when Thomas
Crenshaw the miller doubled as alehouse keeper. By 1789, the
Windmill Inn is noted as 'a very genteel and good accustomed
house, many years in the possession of Mrs Simmonds'. The Windmill
was first leased by Young's in 1848 and the freehold bought in 1899.
Holly Lodge, a small 1888 house at the back, is now run as a hotel by
Young's.

In the pub, which is much larger than the outside suggests, is a huge colour print of J. P. Herring's painting in Tate Britain called *Return From The Derby*. Depicted are horse-drawn coaches stopping for refreshment before covering the last 4 miles to London. The building in the picture is today's inn built in 1729. There are numerous other pictures. In winter, there is sometimes a real fire in one of the two main bars. In summer there are many more visitors and the outdoor tables are popular. Inside bar billiards and dominoes are played here. There is a handsome no-smoking room.

The food includes sandwiches of home-made bread, baguettes, steak and ale pie and various vegetarian dishes. There is also a children's menu. Young's beers are served and there is a long list of wines available by the glass. The Windmill is open all day with food available at lunchtime and all day at weekends. Telephone: 020 8673 4578.

- **HOW TO GET THERE:** The Windmill on the Common is in Clapham Common South Side SW4. The nearest Underground station is Clapham Common (Northern Line). Leave by the Clapham Common exit and turn right to walk down Clapham Common South Side.
- **PARKING:** There is some street parking allowed outside.
- **LENGTH OF THE WALK:** 3 miles. Map: OS Explorer 161 London South. (GR 291748).

THE WALK

1. Turn right out of the pub and go right again at the Windmill Cottage to walk along Windmill Drive. Eagle Pond is over to the left. The bandstand over to the right was made for the 1862 International Exhibition in Kensington which attracted even more visitors than the 1851 Great Exhibition. The two huge buildings on the far side, terraced houses looking like seaside hotels, were built in the 1860s. Hampstead can be seen from the top rooms. Stay on the road crossing the Common to pass Mount Pond, which has an island, and Speakers Corner where you can make a speech between sunrise and sunset.

2. Use the pedestrian crossing to cross The Avenue main road and continue ahead on a path. On reaching Clapham Common West Side turn left. Here there are new buildings and a new road called Walsingham Place. Go through the barriers and turn right into Thurleigh Road. Here the homely Victorian houses are in good repair with many original features.

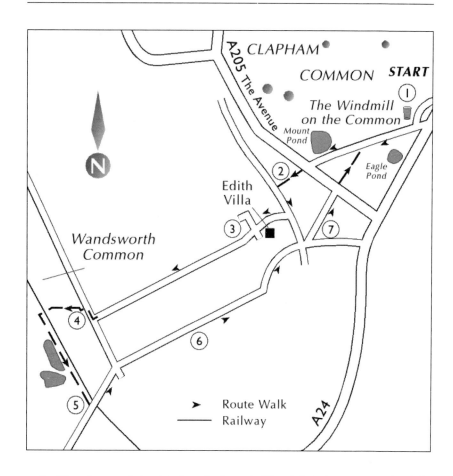

3. After the road double bends there is Thurleigh Avenue on the left. Here, on the left, with its original glass is Edith Villa where cockney music hall comedian Gus Elen lived from 1934 until his death in 1940. One of his songs was 'Wiv a ladder and some glasses/You can see to Hackney Marshes/If it wasn't for the 'ouses in between'. Here he was, to use a local phrase, 'betwixt the Commons'. Continue down Thurleigh Road where there is an interesting mixture of architectural styles and Victorian post boxes. Dominating the street is the Romanesque-style tower of St Luke's church. The interior, an attempt at Lombardy basilica, was completed in 1889 with the landmark campanile added in 1892. The road runs down into the valley of the Falcon Brook which has sources in Streatham and Tooting Bec and joins the Thames at Battersea. The Falcon is running from the left under the road just before the Edward VII post box beyond Montholme Road. Stay in Thurleigh Road as it rises up the far side of the valley to Wandsworth Common.

4. At Bolingbroke Grove go right. Cross on the pedestrian crossing and continue along the road, but after a short distance turn left on the metalled path running onto Wandsworth Common. Follow the way over the railway line carrying Victoria-Brighton trains. On the far side go left at once. Soon the path is between the railway and two large ponds. New duckboards carry a path across the water and fishing remains popular here in season. The path runs ahead to reach a road. Opposite is Wandsworth Common Station.

5. Turn left to cross the railway and follow Nightingale Lane which as a country lane was noted for its nightingales. Beyond the Common the road runs downhill into the Falcon Brook valley. The two streams forming the main brook meet under the road. As the road begins to climb there is Nightingale House on the right. This was the home of Lord Wandsworth (1844–1912) who gave the house as a Home for the Aged Poor of the Jewish Faith in memory of his parents Viscount and Viscountess de Stern.

6. A little further up the hill and on the same side is number 99, Queen Elizabeth House, where preacher Charles Spurgeon of Spurgeon's Tabernacle at the Elephant and Castle fame lived. Next door is the charming Nightingale pub and opposite is a mid-Victorian villa with an Italianate tower. At the top of the hill, on the left and just before Old Park Avenue is number 40 which has a blue plaque commemorating Punch cartoonist H.M. Bateman who lived here from 1910 to 1914. Continue ahead to the Common.

7. Follow Nightingale Walk, which is lined with bollards, across the Common. At the junction with The Avenue main road use the pedestrian crossing and continue on the path opposite. Half-left is a view (better in winter) of Battersea Power Station's four chimneys. The path passes woodland and an enclosure to meet Windmill Drive beyond a gate. Turn right along the road and at the end go left to return to the Windmill on the Common.

⬤6 South Bank
The Rose and Crown

This route explores the streets each side of Blackfriars Road, the boundary between Waterloo and Southwark, and visits St George's Circus which was designed as the climax of the new road from the new Blackfriars Bridge. This was largely open ground until the 19th century when St George's Fields was covered with warehouses and many small houses so robbing the approach to the Elephant and Castle of its rural atmosphere. However, there are still plenty of reminders of earlier days.

The Rose and Crown stands in an area which was once the Paris Garden mentioned by William Shakespeare in his play *Henry VIII*. The name Paris Garden lives on with the street name at the side of the pub and the recently restored Christ Church churchyard is the remains of the huge garden. Hops provide shelter for the outdoor tables where the pub garden merges with the churchyard. This was the edge of the Lambeth Marsh and the first church had to be rebuilt after sinking into the ground. The present church building opened in 1960 as a replacement for the church bombed in the Second World War.

The pub, built in 1887 and replacing an earlier building, has a very homely atmosphere. The walls are crowded Victorian-style with pictures. Many are local views including an old photograph of Blackfriars across the river, a drawing of the Globe Theatre and a half complete Blackfriars Bridge. Some of the pictures are on the stairs which have the feel of a staircase in a 19th-century home leading to bedrooms. At the top there is in fact an airy dining room but the great attraction at the Rose and Crown is eating outside in the summer.

The food, served at lunchtimes, includes bacon, lettuce and tomato sandwiches and baguettes, jacket potatoes, Stilton ploughman's and a range of burgers. This is a Shepherd Neame house serving its own beers along with Tetley's Bitter and Burton Ale. The opening times are 11.30 am to 11 pm Monday to Friday. Telephone: 020 7928 4285. (At weekends the walk can still start from here even though the pub is not open. Refreshment is available every day at the Mad Hatter with its entrance in Southwark Street on the far side of the churchyard. Telephone: 020 7401 9222.)

- **HOW TO GET THERE:** The Rose and Crown is on the corner of Paris Gardens and Colombo Street SE1. Turn left out of Southwark Station (Jubilee Line) to find Colombo Street on the left.
- **PARKING:** There is little street parking in this central London area.
- **LENGTH OF THE WALK:** 2 miles. Map: London street atlas; OS Explorer 173 London North (GR 316803).

THE WALK

1. On leaving the pub's front door turn left past The Rectory to walk along Colombo Street. The name comes from the Paris Garden's 19th-century manor bailiff Alexander Colombo. On the left is the Christ Church garden. At Blackfriars Road turn right. Just before the next turning use the crossing to go left down Nicholson Street at the side of the Prince William Henry pub. Ahead is the Electoral Reform Society which administers professional body and trade union elections.

2. At Chancel Street turn right. The road turns into Dolben Street. The new Brinton Walk houses are on the site of 49 Dolben Street where Mary Wollstonecraft lived from 1788 to 1791 just before writing *Vindication of the Rights of Women.* An original 18th-century street frontage can be seen round the corner on the left. Once in Dolben Street go right into Gambia Street which is to be closed to traffic. Walk

past Mar i Terra bar, the former Hop Pole pub, to go under the railway and reach Union Street.

3. Go down the side of the Lord Nelson opposite to enter Nelson Square. On the side of the flats ahead is a plaque recalling the poet Shelley, Mary Wollstonecraft's son-in-law, living in the square in 1814. Bear left and ahead is a fragment of the original terrace which Shelley would have known as new houses. Keep ahead down the side of the early 19th-century houses to reach Surrey Row – the name recalls that on leaving the huge Paris Garden one would once have been in Surrey and not London. Go left under the railway and then right into Great Suffolk Street. Across the road is a former bacon factory which once provided passersby with a delightful smell of smoking bacon. At once go right into Pocock Street.

St George's Circus

4. Ahead on the corner of Glasshill Street are the gothic-style Drapers' Almshouses built in 1820. Continue past King's Bench Street, recalling the King's Bench Prison which was nearby, to pass the St Alphege House, the former St Alphege church Clergy House designed in distinctive style by William Bucknall and built in 1910 (the site of the original church is passed later). Turn left into Rushworth Street. Continue to the far end of the street and turn right into King James Street.

5. At the crossroads with Lancaster Street the new flats on the left occupy the site of the once well-known St Alphege church built in 1882. The Bridge House pub, rebuilt across the road a decade later in 1894, survives. The street now narrows as it runs alongside 1899 Hunter House, London County Council flats with an interesting frieze above the entrances. At the T-junction go left to a main road, Borough Road. Opposite are the main buildings of South Bank University.

6. Turn right to reach St George's Circus. This is the climax of the road from Blackfriars Bridge which opened in 1769. The obelisk in the middle of the circus is dated 1771. The Georgian houses on the left include Obelisk Dairy, founded in 1810, and still boasting on its frontage 'New milk fresh from the country twice daily'. Turn right up Blackfriars Road to the first crossroads. Turn left along Webber Street. Before the end of the curving street there are Church Commissioners cottages in Ufford Street (right) built in 1901. They were managed by Octavia Hill, the housing pioneer and co-founder of the National Trust, who insisted on the garden opposite being included in the plans.

7. At The Cut the road is alongside the Old Vic theatre which opened in 1818 just before The Cut was dug through Lambeth Marsh. The theatre's foundation stone is on the left just before the corner. On the far (western) side of the theatre is the only urban Millennium Green to be created in 2000. Go ahead down Cornwall Road at the side of the Llewellyn Alexander Gallery. Pass under the Waterloo East railway bridge and right by the baker's to enter Roupell Street. This unspoilt 1820s street of tiny houses has appeared in numerous films and television programmes including *Upstairs Downstairs* and *Dr Who*.

8. At the far end cross Hatfields which is named after the hat trade which flourished here. The Sainsbury family were hatters before opening their grocery in nearby Stamford Street – hence the Mad Hatter pub. The walk continues ahead along Meymott Street. Take the first left into Paris Gardens to find the Rose and Crown.

Borough
The George

7

Borough High Street was once packed with pubs and today many remain on historic sites. The route follows the old main road south before bearing west into narrow streets known to Charles Dickens. The return is by way of Borough Market, London's oldest market.

The George is London's last remaining galleried inn and so special that it is now in the care of the National Trust. It was built in 1677 and soon became a coaching inn. This is how Charles Dickens knew the inn which is featured in his novel *Little Dorrit*. There was certainly an inn on the site in 1542 and probably earlier. In the Tudor period the gate on London Bridge closed at night which meant that travellers arriving late needed accommodation. City merchants bound for the Dover road often crossed the Thames to sleep at a Borough pub to be able to get an early start. In the 18th century there were daily coach services to Dover, Canterbury, Maidstone, Brighton and Hastings. A weekly stage waggon for goods left every Wednesday evening for Tenterden arriving there two days later. Inside the inn today there are still small rooms. Babies and children are welcome as in coaching days.

Food includes sausages and mash, chicken and ham pie with chips, salad, pasta and a vegetarian dish, served from 12 noon to 3 pm. In summer this can be enjoyed in the courtyard, which has the best view of the building. The National Trust has leased the building to Whitbread. Flowers, Greene King and Fuller's ales are available and there is a wide selection of guest beers. The George is open all day. Telephone: 020 7407 2056.

- **HOW TO GET THERE:** The George is on the east side of Borough High Street near the Southwark Street junction. The nearest Underground station is London Bridge (Jubilee and Northern Line).
- **PARKING:** There is little street parking in this central London area and none in Borough High Street.
- **LENGTH OF THE WALK:** $1^1/_2$ miles. Map: London street atlas; OS Explorer 173 London North (GR 327802).

THE WALK

1. Turn left out of the George's gateway. The next old inn yard is Talbot Yard where Copyprints occupies the site of the Tabard Inn where Geoffrey Chaucer sets the opening of *The Canterbury Tales*. The hostelry was the London residence of the Abbot of Hyde in Hampshire but also took guests. The next alley is Queen's Head Yard where the mother of John Harvard was the Queen's Head landlady. Look for the plaque at the front of Mackintosh Duncan on the corner. Harvard's fortune, which allowed him to go to America and found Harvard University, was built on the profits of his mother's pub and his father's nearby butcher's. Continue down the High Street passing more alleys. In Newcomen Street, which grew from Axe and Bottle Yard, is the King's Arms which displays the arms of George II which were once attached to the south gate of London Bridge. In Trinity Court, by the Blue Eyed Maid, is timber-framed Lomax House. Beyond the John Harvard Library the alley looks modern but the brick wall, found on the right a few yards down the turning, is part of the former Marshalsea Debtors' Prison where Charles Dickens' father John was imprisoned between 1823 and 1824. For a time his mother was forced to join her husband.

2. St George's church dates from 1734 but it is the third church on the site. Chaucer knew the brand new second one which later had Henry VIII's lute player as rector. The present building is the scene of Little Dorrit's christening and marriage. Continue ahead at the road junction

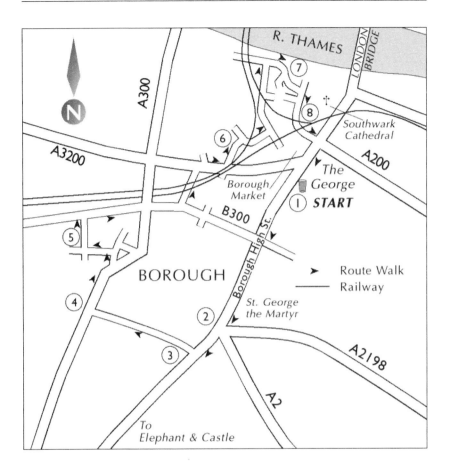

by Borough Underground Station. This was the route for stage coaches leaving the George. The paved surface ceased at Stones' End (by the police station) and after the toll gate the next landmark was the Elephant and Castle.

3. The walk turns right (before the police station) into Lant Street where Dickens lived as a boy when his father was in Marshalsea Prison. The landlord and his wife were the model for Mr and Mrs Garland in *The Old Curiosity Shop* and the lodging is featured in *David Copperfield*. Young Charles took breakfast and supper to his parents in the prison and in between worked at the blacking factory across the river. Pass the Gladstone Arms, with a large portrait of a young looking prime minister, and Charles Dickens School. The author describes the street in *The Pickwick Papers*: 'There is a repose about Lant Street in the

Borough which sheds a gentle melancholy upon the soul. There are also a good many houses to let in the street, it is a bye street too, and its dullness is soothing.' Today the Dickens' association means that it is far from dull. In Sudrey Street, left just before the main road, there can be found the charming Gable Cottages built in 1889 for Octavia Hill's housing association which sought to improve the area.

4. At Southwark Bridge Road cross to the Goldsmiths Arms and turn right. After a short distance is Winchester House built as a workhouse in 1777 but now a Fire Service training centre and museum (open by appointment). Ahead, on the same side of the curving Southwark Bridge Road, is a Welsh Chapel designed in the 1870s by Swansea architect Thomas Thomas. Before the chapel bear left into Great Guildford Street and at once sharp left into Copperfield Street. After a short distance there are the Winchester Cottages built in 1893. The many mentions of Winchester here recall that this area was once part of the Bishop of Winchester's estate. The Diocese of Winchester embraced South London until as recently as the 19th century. Opposite the cottages is a garden on the site of All Hallows' church which was bombed in the Second World War.

5. Turn right into Pepper Street and then go right along Union Street. Cross the main road to go into Flat Iron Square ahead. Turn left down O'Meara Street to pass the Virgin Mary grotto outside the Most Precious Blood church and go under the Charing Cross-London Bridge railway. Use the crossing and go right along Southwark Street and left down Redcross Way. On the corner there is Cromwell Buildings, a block of model Victorian working class flats built after the 1851 Great Exhibition.

6. At Park Street turn right to go under the railway into the street's Georgian climax. Ahead is Southwark Cathedral towering over Borough Market, London's oldest fruit and vegetable market. The buildings date from 1851 and are a hive of activity at night as lorries unload ready for the dawn trading. On Saturdays there is a thriving food market. Turn left down Stoney Street to Clink Street and go right to pass the remains of Winchester Palace's dining hall. Here the Bishop of Winchester entertained Catherine of Aragon on the eve of her first wedding across the river at St Paul's Cathedral. Later Mary I brought her husband Philip of Spain here direct from their wedding at Winchester before facing the hostile crowds in the City of London.

7. Beyond the Golden Hinde replica in St Saviour's Dock, follow the road past Southwark Cathedral. Here Shakespeare's brother is buried between the choir stalls. In the same year Baby John Harvard was baptised here – look for the baptism entry in the register outside the Harvard Chapel. In the nave the bard himself is commemorated with a memorial and window – the figure of Shakespeare is sometimes clasping a spray of rosemary, an emblem of remembrance, mentioned in *Hamlet* and *Romeo and Juliet.* Opposite is a Chaucer window. The building, a former priory church, became a cathedral in 1905 when the Diocese of Southwark was created. Continue along the street which passes through Borough Market to become Bedale Street. The pub and shops here feature in the *Bridget Jones* film. At the main road go right past the Underground entrance to the pedestrian crossing which leads across Southwark Street and Borough High Street. Go right for the George.

ATTRACTION ON THE ROUTE
Southwark Cathedral Exhibition is part of the cathedral's Millennium Project development on the riverside. The Southwark Cathedral Exhibition, A Long View of London, is named after the famous view of London drawn from the tower in 1638 by Dutchman Wenceslas Hollar and features the history of Bankside. Open daily 10 am to 6 pm. The admission charge includes an audio tour of the cathedral. There is no charge for visiting the cathedral church. Telephone: 020 7367 6700.

8 Bermondsey
The Angel

Bermondsey is a riverside community which has remained free of tourists largely due to its inaccessibility until the recent arrival of the Jubilee Line. Visitors would pass through from Southwark to Rotherhithe on a main road which avoids the riverside. The closure of the docks and redevelopment has resulted in long stretches of riverside being opened up as promenade between the remaining warehouses. But the past is not forgotten. Opposite the Angel, and in an attractive setting, are the excavated remains of Edward III's palace. On Bermondsey Wall East, near upstream Cherry Garden Pier, you will find a lifesize sculpture of the former local MP Dr Alfred Salter who in the 20th-century's inter-war years pioneered good health services and model housing. Find his daughter to whom he is waving and the cat on the river wall. This walk goes inland across Southwark Park, then around a vast lake originally dug as a dock, before passing through Rotherhithe village with its Scandinavian seafarer churches.

The name Angel often indicates that a pub was a religious establishment giving shelter to travellers. The Angel on Bermondsey Wall is the successor to a 15th-century inn belonging to nearby Bermondsey Abbey. It was probably called the Salutation at first but for a time it was known as the Moated House after the old palace with its dried up moat opposite. Christopher Jones, Captain of the *Mayflower* from nearby Rotherhithe, bought supplies here for the voyage to America. Captain Cook drank here before setting sail for Australia. The pub featured in Samuel Pepys' famous diary and shortly afterwards Judge Jeffreys became a regular, watching for the executions on the beach across the river at Wapping's Execution Dock. He is said to haunt the balcony. More recent visitors were artists J.M. Whistler and Augustus John.

The present building overhanging the Thames is early 19th century and became the haunt of dockers. The view is spectacular from this spot on a river bend with Tower Bridge and St Paul's Cathedral upstream and Rotherhithe and Limehouse downstream. It has a special link with navigation for every ship passing upstream must sound a hooter here to request the opening of Tower Bridge. The bar in the Angel is in the shape of a barge's hull and the walls have plenty of old local photographs.

This pub has a very good reputation for food. Bar snacks include home-made soup, cockles and mussels with brown bread and wild boar sausages as well as baps with various fillings. This is now a Greenall's house with a wide selection of ales including Worthington's Best and Murphy's and guest beers in summer. Open all day with food served from 12 noon to 1.45 pm and weekday evenings. Telephone: 020 7237 3608.

- **HOW TO GET THERE:** The Angel is in riverside Bermondsey Wall East SE16. The nearest station is Bermondsey (Jubilee Line). Turn right along Jamaica Road, left down Cherry Garden Street and right at the river.
- **PARKING:** There is a small car park opposite.
- **LENGTH OF THE WALK:** 2 miles. Map: OS Explorer 161 London South (GR 349798).

THE WALK

1. Turn left out of the pub to reach a tall lonely riverside building. This was a lighterage office looking after barges. Today it is important as,

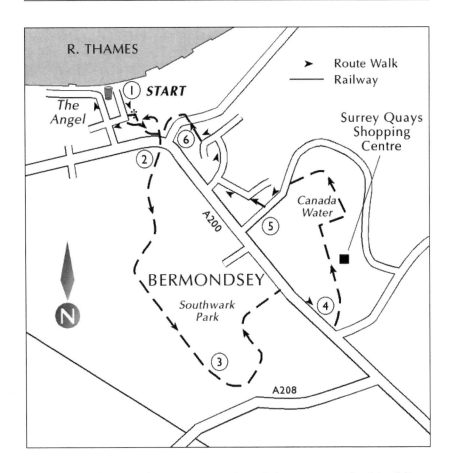

along with the Angel, it is a reminder of the many packed buildings which blocked the river view. Among the houses in the gap immediately downstream was a flat occupied by Lord Snowdon who entertained his future wife Princess Margaret there. Turn right into Fulford Street to walk down to St Peter's Church in Paradise Street. The walk continues ahead by the church through gates. Follow the path and turn left to walk through a park and reach the main road. Turn left to the traffic lights to cross the road.

2. Once on the far side go ahead into Southwark Park which opened in 1869 on the site of market gardens. Today it is known for its Café Gallery. Go ahead and take the left hand path. Keep ahead at the next two junctions, passing the water fountain in memory of temperance advocate Jebez West, to walk alongside the bowling green. Bear right

The view from the pub

and left to join the path along the west side. Cross a park road and keep ahead down a straight avenue. Over to left there is a glimpse of the lake. Soon, on the right, there is the redundant Clare College Chapel built in 1911 as the Cambridge College's mission church.

3. Continue on the path as it bends round to the left. Keep on past the gates and Sports Complex. At a junction bear right to reach a main road – Lower Road. Turn right to pass the Caulkers pub which is named after those who made ships watertight. The docks were once across the road. Cross left over Lower Road and continue along the road for a few yards to turn left into Surrey Quays built on dockland.

4. Go over to the shopping centre and turn left. Walk the length of the building (right) which contains Tesco and Bhs. At the far end bear right to walk round Canada Water which is the remains of the much larger Canada Dock where Canadian timber was unloaded. Cross the bridge over the Albion Channel and stay by Canada Water to reach the entrance to Canada Water Station. Keep forward down the road to pass the former Dock Offices.

5. Here cross at the crossing to go right through a garden. On the far side continue along Moodkee Street. Go right into Neptune Street to pass the Cock and Monkey. The road bends to meet Albion Street opposite the Norske Kirke – the Norwegian church built in 1927, with a typical Scandinavian spire, to serve Norwegian sailors and still a centre for Norwegians in Britain. Go left to St Olave's Square which was opened by Crown Prince Harald of Norway. Note the public lavatories where notices are in Norwegian: Maend (men) and Kvinder (women). The Finnish and Swedish churches are nearby.

6. Go right to cross the entrance to the Rotherhithe Tunnel, built in 1904–8, and go ahead to cross Brunel Road – the main entrance to Rotherhithe village. Go left towards the roundabout and then right into King's Stairs Gardens. Take the left fork and follow the way down to St Peter's church and Paradise Street. Go left past the church and Fulford Street to the next junction. Here is number 23 which was once a police station and the model for the television series *Dixon of Dock Green*. The blue lamp is now white. Go right down Cathay Street at the side. The Angel is ahead.

Dulwich Village
The Crown and Greyhound

Dulwich has a rural air with village shops, a thriving pub, signposts, a tollgate, a church and a famous school. It is the school, Dulwich College, which has preserved the area. In 1605 actor Edward Alleyn, who organised bear baiting on Bankside and knew William Shakespeare, purchased the Manor of Dulwich. In 1619 he endowed the school, the College of God's Gift at Dulwich, for ten scholars. By the middle of the 19th century the estate was wealthy enough to expand the school which became Dulwich College with fine buildings and grounds. The Estate Governors still pursue a policy of conservation and this walk embraces both the village, College and, by way of the tollgate, the remarkable woodland.

The Crown and Greyhound is in the heart of Dulwich almost alongside the burial ground consecrated in 1616 by Archbishop Abbot (see Walk 14) watched by Edward Alleyn. The present pub is the successor to the Crown on this site and the Greyhound which stood opposite until 1895. The Greyhound was the grand inn with a ballroom and the London-Sevenoaks coach stopping daily. There was some surprise when the small Crown bought the large Greyhound. The present magnificent building was completed in 1898. The Greyhound site is now marked by Pickwick Road. Charles Dickens often dined there with the Dulwich Club and as a result he made Dulwich the retirement village for Mr Pickwick.

Today's pub, just called the Dog by villagers, remains as popular with visitors as the old Greyhound. There are four bars including one non-smoking. The original mahogany counters remain, there are doors with etched glass announcing 'Billiard Room' and the fires have real flames. The old photographs include one of the Greyhound and the Dulwich Tollgate. In summer the large garden is an attraction with its horse chestnut tree. Children are welcome and enjoy the family facilities in the conservatory and the outdoor sandpit. At the same time the building remains a popular venue for wedding receptions.

Food includes Emmental and egg rolls, large sandwiches, toasted sandwiches and specials including steak and kidney pie and herb fish cakes. There is always a vegetarian dish such as vegetable moussaka. This is an Allied Domecq house with Burton Ale, Tetley's, Young's, Castlemaine and specials such as Morland Old Speckled Hen. The pub is open all day with the menu available from 12 noon to 2.45 pm and 5.30 pm to 11 pm. Telephone: 020 8693 2466.

- **HOW TO GET THERE:** The Crown and Greyhound is in the Dulwich main street, called just Dulwich Village SE21, south of the A2214 Village Way, east of Herne Hill. The nearest station is Dulwich North. Turn left along Red Post Hill to reach Dulwich Village beyond the crossroads.
- **PARKING:** There is some street parking allowed outside.
- **LENGTH OF THE WALK:** 3^1/$_2$ miles. Map: OS Explorer 161 London South (GR 332741).

THE WALK

1. Turn left to walk past the shops and Pickwick Road (right). To the left are several 18th-century houses. At the junction ahead there is the tiny Grammar School building designed by Charles Barry of Houses of Parliament fame. At the road fork is the Dulwich College Chapel and the College's oldest buildings.

2. Keep ahead, to the left of the chapel, to follow College Road. Beyond the chapel there is Dulwich Picture Gallery, England's oldest public gallery with a collection dating from 1626 (see below). Go over

the crossroads by the Mill Pond to pass the main Dulwich College buildings. The foundation stone was laid in 1866 and the completed building by Charles Barry the Younger was opened by the Prince of Wales. Former pupils include explorer Ernest Shackleton and author P.G. Woodhouse. Keep forward to pass through the tollgate which dates from 1789 when the road provided access to grazing land. Pedestrians pass through free but a board gives a list of pre-decimal charges: motor car 6d; sheep, lambs and hogs 2$\frac{1}{2}$d per score and a donkey 3d. Continue up College Road to Sydenham Hill Station and St Stephen's church which was completed in 1875. The *Trial and Stoning of St Stephen* was painted onto the wet plaster in 1872 by Sir Edward Poynter. Opposite the station turn left to follow the steep path, Low Cross Wood Lane, up Sydenham Hill.

45

3. At the top there is Dulwich Wood House, an Italianate Victorian villa which has become a Young's pub, and is open all day. Go right and left to walk along the main road. Turn left into Crescent Wood Road. On the corner is a Camberwell boundary stone and today this is the boundary between the London Borough of Southwark, which now embraces Camberwell, and the London Borough of Lewisham. Walk along the side road to pass a pillar box and go through a kissing gate (right) into Sydenham Hill Wood.

4. The wood is a nature reserve managed by the London Wildlife Trust. Take the first turning on the left to follow the path across the top of the railway tunnel and down onto the valley floor to see into the (blocked up) tunnel. Walk away from the tunnel to follow the path on the old trackbed. Where the way ends go left up steps and bear round to the right. In winter there is a view through the trees towards Westminster – the London Eye Millennium Wheel on the South Bank can usually be seen. Go through the kissing gate. Do not cross the bridge but continue ahead down the wide Cox's Walk. At the far end there is the (Harvester) Grove Tavern. To the right is St Peter's church which has tower and spire erected in 1885, paid for by F.J. Horniman of tea fame.

5. Turn left along Dulwich Common road – a medieval lane. After a short distance go right into Dulwich Park which opened in 1890 on former farmland. Bear left to follow a park road. After a junction there is a lake over to the right and nearby a Barbara Hepworth sculpture. Stay on the road to reach Old College Gate. Turn right to reach the Crown and Greyhound.

ATTRACTION ON THE ROUTE

Dulwich Picture Gallery has a collection dating from 1626. The building, by Sir John Soane, opened in 1817 as the country's first public gallery. The core of the collection was assembled for the King of Poland but when he was forced to abdicate the delivery was halted and eventually made available to the British public. Today the 300 strong collection on show includes works by Rembrandt, Rubens and Van Dyck. Open Monday to Friday, 10 am (Saturday 11 am; Sunday 2 pm) to 5 pm. Admission charge. Telephone: 020 8693 8000.

⑩ Blackheath
The Princess of Wales

Blackheath, which may have been bleak heath, is now a vast expanse of grass crossed by Watling Street. In 1381 Wat Tyler assembled the Peasants' Revolt here and in 1450 the Cade Rebellion led by Jack Cade also rallied here. Between these two events Henry V arrived in triumph from the Battle of Agincourt in 1415. Henry VIII came to meet his new wife Anne of Cleves who he found less attractive than her portrait which had appealed to him. Today there are fun fairs on the heath at Easter and in the summer. This walk takes you over Blackheath and to a splendid viewpoint in Greenwich Park, returning past the deer enclosure.

The Princess of Wales, which has a fine Georgian-style frontage with a large window, is a delightful mid-Victorian building. However, the pub does date from the Georgian period having opened in 1806. The view from the front bar is of the heath where in summer drinks are enjoyed on the grass – but only if you ask for a plastic glass. At the back there is a conservatory with a tented ceiling and a garden. One corridor has a number of pictures relating to Queen Caroline who is the pub's

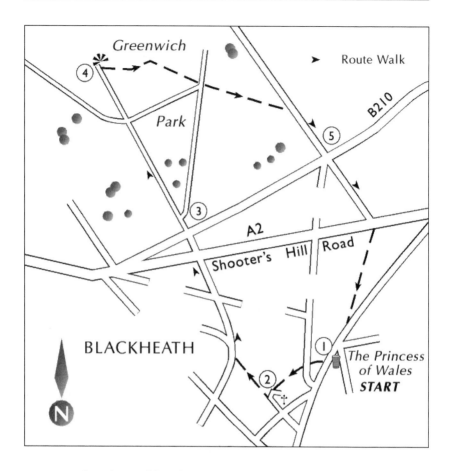

Princess of Wales and lived nearby. (For some time in the last century the sign outside wrongly depicted Queen Alexandra.) The pictures include Caroline's wedding when she married the Prince Regent at St James's Palace; the watermen demonstrating in her support outside her riverside house at Hammersmith and Caroline as Queen leaving the House of Lords in triumph. Her husband, as George IV, had barred her from the Coronation and unsuccessfully sought a divorce in the House of Lords. A plaque outside the pub, and a dedicated corner inside, recall that the Blackheath Rugby Football Club, the world's oldest Rugby Union Football Club, was founded here in 1858.

For lunch, baked potatoes and fish and chips are always available and sometimes steak and ale pie is on the specials menu. There are also several puddings. This is a Bass house with a wide range of beers available. The pub is open all day with food served at lunchtimes. Telephone: 020 8852 6881.

- **HOW TO GET THERE:** The Princess of Wales is in Montpelier Row SE3 on the south side of Blackheath. Bus 192 from Blackheath Station stops nearby.
- **PARKING:** There is little provision nearby as this is on the edge of Blackheath village.
- **LENGTH OF THE WALK:** 1^1/$_2$ miles. Map: OS Explorer 161 London South or 162 Greenwich and Gravesend (GR 398764).

THE WALK

1. Turn left out of the pub to cross the pedestrian crossing. Bear half-left on the path running across the heath towards the church. There is a road to cross before All Saints is reached. The church was built like a model, complete with spire, on the heath in the 1850s. The architect was Benjamin Ferrey but it became famous as the parish church of hostage Terry Waite who was prayed for here during his long years in captivity.

2. At the church take the footpath which leads to an isolated group of houses at Blackheath Vale where there was once a windmill. Here bear slightly right on a wider path which includes a cycleway. Continue over a junction with Long Pond Road and cross the main Shooter's Hill Road at the lights. Ahead are the gates of Greenwich Park. Look to the right to see in the wall a memorial of the Cornish leaders who led a rebellion to here against taxation in 1497 and were executed.

3. Walk ahead into Greenwich Park and down the Royal Park's wide avenue to reach the viewpoint at General Wolfe's statue. From here there is a view across the buildings of the former Royal Naval College to the Canary Wharf skyscrapers on the Isle of Dogs. To the west is Central London and north-east is the Dome.

4. From the viewpoint turn right to take the path just before the refreshment kiosk. Follow the way to reach the remains of Queen Elizabeth's Oak. It was planted in the 12th century and finally collapsed in 1991. Elizabeth I is said to have danced round the tree which was so large that it may have been used as a lock up for those who broke park regulations. The new oak was planted in 1992 by Baron Greenwich – better known as Prince Philip. Turn right and keep ahead over a wide walk to pass along the side of the Flower Garden. At the gate in the wall go right along the road. To the left are Vanbrugh Pits, the grassy

View of the Isle of Dogs from Greenwich Park

remains of the heath's gravel pits and a place to find blue harebells blooming in the summer. Over the wall (right) is the deer enclosure.

5. At the road junction cross over to take the road (a continuation of Maze Hill) to the left of the Andrew Webb Drinking Fountain. At the far end go over the crossing and follow the path across the heath to Prince of Wales Road opposite the pond. Turn right for the Princess of Wales.

11 Shooter's Hill
The Bull

This walk is on a viewpoint, 432 feet above sea level, which formerly divided Greater London from Kent. The main road is Watling Street and it was once the pilgrim road to and from Canterbury and the main route from the port of Dover. In 'A Tale of Two Cities', Charles Dickens describes the Dover mail coach coming up the hill. Byron also wrote about the hill which remains remarkably rural and wooded. Among the houses there is even a pre-Roman burial mound. This was a haunt of highwaymen who came out of the woods. The summit had a gallows last used in Trafalgar year, 1805. Earlier Samuel Pepys wrote: 'I rode under a man that hangs at Shooters Hill and a filthy sight to see how the flesh is shrunk from his bones.' The walk starts off through parkland north of the main road, with fine views, and continues into woodland to the south.

The Bull was built in 1881 by Beasley's Brewery of nearby Plumstead. This red brick pub replaced the much larger Georgian building which stood adjacent at this strategic point at the top of the hill from 1749 and fed both travellers and those who came to see the executions. It was a rambling building with a room at the very top for enjoying the view. The original William Hickey mentions the old Bull in his memoirs published in 1761. An even earlier inn is mentioned by Daniel Defoe in 1687. A former landlady claimed that the pub was haunted.

Behind the door in the back bar can be found some pictures of the old building. There is a pool table and occasional live music. Outside, but hidden from the road, there is an unspoilt garden. Families are welcome.

This is a Courage house with Young's beers also available. The Bull is open all day and home-cooked food is served Monday to Saturday at lunchtime. Telephone: 020 8856 0691.

- **HOW TO GET THERE:** The Bull is at the top of Shooter's Hill SE18 on the A207 east of Blackheath. Bus 192 from Blackheath Station stops nearby.
- **PARKING:** There is some parking in side roads but not on the main road.
- **LENGTH OF THE WALK:** 1¹/₂ miles. Map: OS Explorer 162 Greenwich and Gravesend (GR 437765).

THE WALK

1. Turn left out of the pub to walk along the main road. Soon there is the mounting block which indicates the position of the old Bull. Stand on the top and look west to see the London Eye Millennium Wheel. Cross a side road to pass below the landmark brick water tower, built in 1910, which can be seen from Tower Bridge in central London. The hill has long played a role in the capital's communications and the radio and television transmitters succeed a 16th-century beacon and 18th-century shutter telegraph. Ahead a view opens out over Welling in the London Borough of Bexley.

2. Turn left into Eaglesfield Road to pass through parkland. To the right a magnificent view of Kent opens out. The QE2 Bridge near Dartford can be seen to the north-east. At steps (left) bear half-left on a metalled path across Eaglesfield Recreation Ground. The name is derived from the eagles on the shield of an 18th-century High Sheriff of Kent. This is a former garden and the small children's play area has replaced a pond which is the hill's highest point. The path leads to a crossroads. Go left down Foxcroft Road. Ahead is Shrewsbury Lane which is named after the Earl of Shrewsbury who built a mansion over to the right in 1789. A decade later this (now replaced) house with a

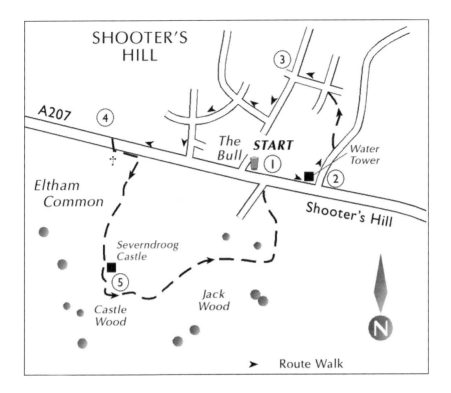

view became the home of Princess Charlotte, daughter of the Prince Regent. Across Shrewsbury Lane is the entrance to Occupation Lane and a glimpse of the view west.

3. Go left into Shrewsbury Lane. When the high pavement ends turn right into Ankerdine Crescent. Ahead is a panoramic view of the Thames and central London. The Millennium Dome is in the foreground with the tall City of London buildings beyond. Before the bottom of the hill take the high path on the left which curves round above Moordown (road). Below can be seen the towers of Woolwich Barracks. As the path curves the Thames Barrier comes into view. In winter the pointed roof of the Rotunda in Woolwich, which once stood in St James's Park, can be seen. At the next road junction turn left up Donaldson Road to the main road. Here go right on the raised pavement running downhill to a shop and the Red Lion. Cross the main road to Christ Church, a small village-style church, completed in 1856, where a milestone in the churchyard indicates 8 miles to London Bridge.

Shooter's Hill water tower

4. Now turn uphill past a rustic shelter and go right on a metalled lane running into Castle Wood. Continue past Castle House Lodge and at a junction go ahead to Severndroog Castle. The 60 foot high triangular folly was built in 1784 by the widow of Sir William James to mark his capture of Severndroog Castle off the Malabar coast.

5. Just beyond the castle go to a flight of steps where there is a view across Eltham. In one of the houses below Bob Hope was born in 1903. The trees to the right mark the site of Well Hall, home to St Thomas More's daughter Margaret Roper in the 16th century and Edith Nesbit, author of *The Railway Children*, in the 19th century. The spire of Eltham church pinpoints the High Street. Go down the steps and at the bottom turn left to Rose Cottage. Continue on the rough path through Jack Wood following the yellow London Loop waymarks. When the path becomes metalled take the right fork as indicated. The way leads into Crown Woods Lane. At Kenilworth Gardens go right to the main road. Opposite is the mounting block. Turn left to find the Bull across the road.

12 Mottingham
The Porcupine

Mottingham is a village now in the London Borough of Bromley although historically it is linked to Eltham where this walk passes the palace. In medieval times both Mottingham and Eltham were outside London but even today the setting of the former royal palace is farmland with a fine view to the heart of the capital. The walk provides a very good view of Eltham Palace but a visit to the grounds and interior will make a full day out.

The Porcupine's 'Tudor' building dates from only 1922 but there has been a Porcupine pub in the village since the 17th century. The typical Kent weatherboarded building, with a wooden horse trough outside, was taken down by attaching chains to traction engines. It collapsed 'like a pack of cards'. The name may have come from a crest on a coat of arms but 'porcupine' is also the name of a mashing machine used in brewing.

There are two bars. The main one on the left is large with several old photographs on the panelled walls. At the back there is a covered sun terrace overlooking the surprisingly large garden which has not only a small dovecote with doves flying in and out but plenty of climbing frames and garden furniture for children on the lawn. There is also an aviary and some rabbits.

The pub is not only noted for its child provision but also for its very good value food. The all day menu is extensive and includes fish and chips, burgers, baps and jacket potatoes. The biggest breakfast consists of two jumbo sausages, two eggs, three rashers of bacon and chips. The Porcupine is a Scottish and Newcastle house with Courage and John Smith's ale available. It is open all day with food served until about 9.30 pm. Telephone: 020 8857 6901.

- **HOW TO GET THERE:** The Porcupine is in the centre of Mottingham opposite the prominent war memorial. The village is on the A208 at the junction of Court Road and Mottingham Road SE9. The nearest station is Mottingham ('Dartford Loop' line from Charing Cross). Turn right at road and go right at T-junction.
- **PARKING:** There is a car park for pub patrons.
- **LENGTH OF THE WALK:** 2 miles. Map: OS Explorer 162 Greenwich and Gravesend (GR 421729).

THE WALK

1. Turn left out of the pub forecourt passing the pub sign and the war memorial. At the crossroads go right along Mottingham Lane. At the start of the lane there is Eltham College to the left with its Italianate tower built in 1856. Former students include novelist Mervyn Peake and Eric Liddell of *Chariots of Fire* fame. Just beyond Mottingham Gardens (right) there is a footpath (right) with a Green Chain waymark. Only to see W.G. Grace's house (see Walk 13) continue along the lane. There are several interesting Victorian houses and Mottingham Farm, a former dairy farm where today horses are stabled. Fairmount, where the cricketer lived at the end of his life, is on the right just round the bend.

2. The main walk continues to the right by the Green Chain waymark and past the barriers and down the footpath known as King John's Walk. The name may refer to King John II of France who was exiled at Eltham Palace in 1364. The way is gently downhill and soon there is a field on the left. At the end cross, with great care, the A20 dual carriageway and continue ahead to where St John's Path crosses the Dartford Loop railway line at a footbridge. On the far side the path runs

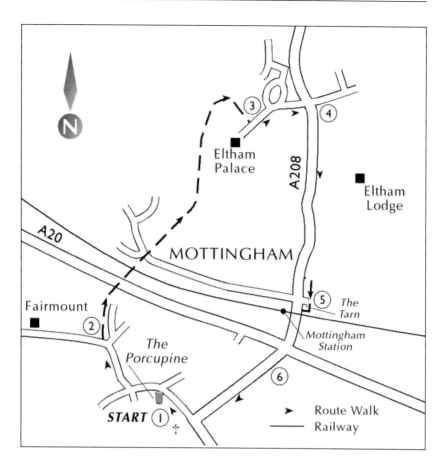

gently up to another road. Beyond here the path is fenced but uphill between fields. As the path levels out the panoramic view to the left opens out. From south to north can be seen the Crystal Palace mast, Battersea Power Station, the London Eye Millennium Wheel, the BT Tower, St Paul's Cathedral, the City's NatWest Tower, Canary Wharf and the Dome. Nearby is Shooter's Hill. Ahead, and peeping through the trees in winter, is the great hall of Eltham Palace. Follow the path which, beyond a gate, passes a stables. At a junction go right up the wide slope to find the bridge spanning the palace moat.

3. In the 14th-century, Eltham Palace was described as 'a very magnificent palace which the King possessed seven miles from London'. Under Richard II Geoffrey Chaucer supervised improvements. In 1402 Henry IV was married here by proxy to Joan of Navarre and in 1415 Henry V came here from France after his triumph at the Battle of Agincourt. The splendid Great Hall, built in 1479, has England's third largest hammerbeam roof. At Christmas 1515 Cardinal Wolsey was made Lord Chancellor in the chapel by Henry VIII. The palace and its adjacent Thirties house, added as a residence by the Courtauld family in 1933, have recently been restored by English Heritage. Do not be tempted through the double green gates above the moat – the attractive path leads to the car park. Turn left to walk away from the bridge with the timber-framed Lord Chancellor's Lodgings to the left. At a junction go sharp right past The Gatehouse to enter Tiltyard Approach. Pass the gateway to The Tiltyard (right) and follow the long high brick wall.

4. At the crossroads go right along Court Road. Here there are several interesting Victorian houses. Soon on the right is the entrance to the Royal Blackheath Golf Club. The badge shows St Andrew, the patron saint of Scotland, since it was the courtiers of James VI of Scotland who introduced golf when the King also became James I of England. By then Eltham Palace had given way to the larger and more popular Greenwich Palace near flat Blackheath where the club was founded five years later in 1608. The Royal Blackheath moved here in 1923 and now uses Eltham Lodge built by Sir John Shaw in 1664. He had bought Eltham Palace but decided to build a new house for himself on the site of a keeper's cottage in the parkland. Continue along the road to The Tarn park on the left.

5. At The Tarn go through the first gate and down the steps to see the brick ice house dating from about 1760. Ice from the pond, then known as Starbucks Pond, was stored here for use at Eltham Lodge. In cold weather villagers were allowed to skate on the frozen pond. Go sharp right to pass the end of the pond and rejoin the road at the far end. Opposite is Mottingham Station. Go left to continue along Court Road crossing the railway and the main road.

6. Soon there is St Andrew's on the left. The village's brick church was not built until 1880 as the Mottingham hamlet had been part of the manor of Eltham since 1290. Only the coming of the railway in 1866, which attracted new housing, caused a new parish to be created. At the T-junction go right for the Porcupine.

13 South Norwood
The Dr W.G. Grace

South Norwood has always been worth a visit for its remarkable cemetery which is the resting place for some famous figures from the fields of church and invention. The name of cricketer W.G. Grace, whose tomb is the most visited, now adorns the pub. Beyond the burial ground, laid out for nearby Beckenham when this was countryside, is now reclaimed countryside. Norwood Country Park has delightful paths, a lake with an island and high ground for viewing not just south London but also the new Tramlink which passes through from Croydon.

The Dr W.G. Grace is a large modern pub named after the famous cricketer who is buried on the opposite side of the tram line. The 'Dr' addition is a reminder that he was a medical doctor and surgeon. In fact he was known simply as 'WG' to the public and, with his distinctive black beard, was one of the few easily recognisable famous faces. He lived from 1818 to 1915 at a time when even members of the Royal Family and cabinet ministers could walk about the streets without being noticed.

Grace was a first rate bowler and fielder as well as a batsman. In 1876 he was 400 not out. He took nearly 300 wickets, made 54,896 runs and played in 22 Test Matches. His last game of cricket was in 1914 – the year before he died at his home in Mottingham (Walk 12).

The pub building would appear modern to Grace but it does resemble a cricket pavilion with steps up to the front door. The inside is filled with pictures of W.G. Grace and cricketing memorabilia including bats, stumps and a ball. A Colman's Mustard advertisement featuring a W.G. Grace figure indicates his wide appeal. There is even a handwritten record of Grace's 126 centuries – he had made a hundred centuries by 1895. The one long bar faces a raised seating area from where, if there was a lawn rather than a road outside, you could watch a game.

This is a Courage house and open all day with food always available. On the changing menu chicken Kiev and cajun chicken curry often feature along with chocolate fudge cake. Bar snacks include the popular dish, lasagne, and there is a specials board. Telephone: 020 8778 4269.

- **HOW TO GET THERE:** The W.G. Grace is in Witham Road which runs south from the A214 Elmers End Road. The Birkbeck Tramlink stop is next door.
- **PARKING:** There is car parking off the main road.
- **LENGTH OF THE WALK:** 2 miles. Map: OS Explorer 161 London South (GR 354690).

THE WALK

1. Turn right out of the pub and walk under the Tramlink bridge. After a short distance go right into Beckenham Cemetery.

2. Continue through the cemetery. Where the road divides go right. To see the W.G. Grace tomb at once bear right again on a curving path, and turn right (but not sharp right) onto a grass path. After a short distance the very well maintained Grace tomb can be seen on the right. There is a huge white cross at the head and bails, ball and bat depicted at the foot. Speaking at the 75th anniversary memorial service, cricket commentator Christopher Martin-Jenkins described the interment: 'The great man was buried on a dark and miserable afternoon in 1915 whilst the terrible Battle of Mons was at its height.' A few yards further on is the recently restored grave of Frederick York Wolsley, inventor of the sheep shearing machine. Retrace the way to the main driveway. The

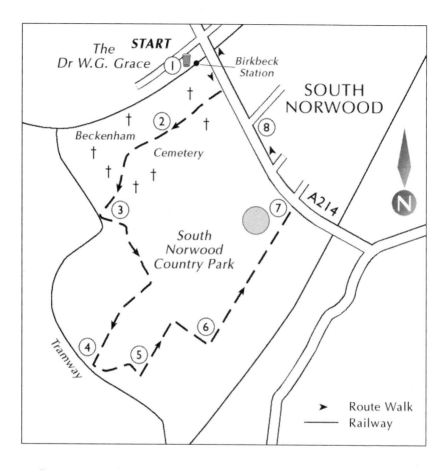

walk continues through the cemetery passing the chapel (left). On the right, just beyond the car park, is the grave of Fr Arthur Tooth (1839–1931) who was imprisoned in 1876 having been charged under the Public Worship Regulation Act for excessive ritual at St James's Hatcham. It was a celebrated case and although he became a hero to many he never sought another benefice and instead lived in his own Christian community in Croydon until 1924. Other famous people buried here include William Walker, the diver who saved Winchester Cathedral from being undermined by a rising water table, and Thomas Crapper, of water closet fame. Stay on the main path as it winds down to the south gate by Harrington Road Tramlink stop.

3. Cross the line to pass the now isolated lodge. At once turn left to follow a footpath back across the line and enter South Norwood

Country Park. This area was once a pottery and brickworks. Later the land was designated as Croydon's sewage farm but this proved unsuccessful due to the clay soil and the works closed in 1967. Now this is once again countryside, attracting an increasing number of birds. At least six species of warbler breed here including reed and sedge warblers. Marsh warblers have also been recorded. Woodpeckers and red kite can also be seen. Take the right hand path. At a junction keep ahead and at the next divide keep right. The path soon runs alongside a pitch and putt course (right) and through a gateway. Keep along the park road and past a visitors centre.

4. Ahead is a Tramlink level crossing. Do not cross the line but bear left across the cobbles and onto a footpath. After a short distance take the left fork and climb up the steep slope (there are a few steps near the top) to the viewpoint.

5. At the viewpoint there is a view north across Penge with church towers and spires standing out. North-east is Shooter's Hill. Looking south, across the tramlink can be seen the tall buildings of Croydon. To the west are the two radio and television masts at Crystal Palace and Beaulieu Heights. Turn right (to the east) and walk down to the end of the mound and descend the steps. Turn left along a path running north. To the right is Rylands Field used for games. Ignore all turnings and follow the path until it bears right. A path runs in a straight line south with drainage ditches on both sides. At the far end go over the footbridge and turn left.

6. Here the path is alongside a stream. Through the trees to the right there is a glimpse of the new Tesco building at Elmers End. At a path junction go left on a path which bends. At a five-way junction go ahead over a bridge. Here the path is more wooded and close to the lake (left). Bear right at the far end and look for access to the lake on the left.

7. There are seats on the jetty. Here waterfowl can often be seen. There may be a kingfisher and waders have occasionally been recorded. Snipe winter in the wet meadow. Beyond here look for a path on the right which leads to a park entrance.

8. Turn left to walk along Elmers End Road which climbs up to Birkbeck Station and the Dr W.G. Grace.

⑭ Croydon
The Dog and Bull

Croydon has become known for its tall buildings which have helped to transform this former Surrey coaching town. So dramatic has been the change that the town has been shortlisted for City status. However, some of the 'new' buildings are now part of our architectural history whilst hidden and largely unknown Old Croydon survives with its palace and church in a green oasis. This is the heart of 16th-century Croydon known to Archbishop Whitgift whose name lives on with the school, shopping centre and almshouses. John Whitgift, a favourite of Elizabeth I, crowned James 1 and attended the Hampton Court Conference which led to the publication of the Authorised Version of the Bible. The walk also visits St Michael's which John Betjeman described as 'one of Pearson's loveliest churches'.

The Dog and Bull is an 18th-century listed building and a busy market pub with fruit and vegetable stalls outside. This has been a market area for 700 years and once operated under a charter from the Archbishop of Canterbury who lived at nearby Croydon Palace.

The bar is in the centre of the small house. Tankards hang from the beams and the walls have framed pictures of early Croydon. One old photograph shows tram lines with a horse-drawn tram in the distance. There is also a large photograph of Prince Charles taken when he visited The Dog and Bull in 1995. Modern additions include a big television screen. In summer there is a surprise back yard recently opened to drinkers.

Food is served at weekday lunchtimes in this award-winning pub and there is a non-smoking area for diners wanting to eat away from the bar. Specials can include sweet and sour pork with rice and salad. There are always the Dog and Bull curry specials. Baguettes include brunch and sausage. Vegetarian pasta bake and Veggie Nachos Grande are always on the menu. The large range of good sandwiches include honey roast ham, turkey and tuna. This is a Young's house with a good range of beers and it is open all day. Telephone: 020 8688 3664.

- **HOW TO GET THERE:** The Dog and Bull is in Surrey Street which runs between Millets in the High Street and the bottom of Crown Hill. George Street is the nearest Tramlink stop.
- **PARKING:** There are thirteen car parks in central Croydon. All are signposted and the nearest to the Dog and Bull is Wandle Street near the flyover.
- **LENGTH OF THE WALK:** 2 miles. Map: OS Explorer 161 London South (GR 323655).

THE WALK

1. Turn left at the pub front door to walk along Surrey Street to the junction. Go left along Church Street which bends. At The Gun Tavern go left again into Old Palace Road leading to Croydon Palace. Cross Church Road where (to the right) Gothic Villas stand on the site of the Archbishop's stables.

2. Beyond the 14th-century great hall (right with an English Heritage sign) look through the school gateway to see more of Croydon Palace. This was the Archbishop of Canterbury's first stop on the way from Lambeth Palace to Canterbury. There were other residences at Otford, Wrotham, Maidstone and Charing for the five day journey. Cardinal Morton, of Morton's Fork fame, twice entertained Henry VII here. Archbishop Whitgift welcomed Elizabeth I and Archbishop Abbot (see Walk 9), who clashed with James I, died here. Archbishop Laud was fond of Croydon and during the Cromwell years, which followed the

Route Walk

Lunar House

Whitgift Shopping Centre

CROYDON

START
The
Dog & Bull

Fairfield
Halls

Croydon
Palace

Archbishop's execution, Croydon suffered less damage than other episcopal palaces. Croydon Palace continued to be the primate's residence until 1780. Turn right into Howley Road which is named after William Howley, Archbishop from 1828 to 1848, who lived at Addington Palace (see Walk 16) and continued to wear the once fashionable wig long after the Georgian era. At the main road, which acts like a wall to Old Croydon, turn right by the garden and churchyard to reach the soaring tower of the parish church.

3. There are five Archbishops buried in Croydon church. The fine recumbent figure of Archbishop Whitgift, who liked Croydon Palace more than his other six palaces, can be seen on his tomb in a chapel. Beyond the church is the Rose and Crown and Ramsey Court, built in the 19th century as almshouses by a foundation dating back to 1447.

Croydon Palace

Continue ahead across the end of Church Road and Church Street into Drummond Road. This runs uphill until it narrows and enters pedestrian only North End. Look up on the right above Oasis to see the old shop building whose architecture is repeated nearby.

4. Turn left along North End. Over to the right is the Whitgift Shopping Centre which stands on the original site of Whitgift School founded by the Archbishop. Continue along the wide shopping walk until meeting traffic. Here go right into Poplar Walk at the side of Marks and Spencer.

5. Ahead on the left is the towering building of St Michael's church which is noted as one of London's finest parish churches. The foundation stone was laid in 1880 by Horatio, the 3rd Lord Nelson. The architect was John Loughborough Pearson who was responsible for many fine Victorian churches including Truro Cathedral. According to architectural historian Nikolaus Pevsner the Croydon interior 'is one of the most satisfying of its date anywhere'. The church is open on weekdays as well as for Sunday services at 11 am and 6.30 pm. At Wellesley Road ahead go right. This road is a wide dual carriageway with trams running down the centre. Here are some of Croydon's noted new buildings.

6. Immediately on the left is the 20 storey Lunar House designed by Denis Crump and Partners for the reclusive property tycoon Harry

Hyams who chose the name. It is now occupied by the Home Office immigration department. The site of Lunar House and nearby Apollo House was previously occupied by Croydon High School for Girls. Opposite an entrance to the Whitgift Centre (right) is Lansdowne Road. Here is a Nineties post modern building, Lansdowne House by Richard Seifert, built on the site of one of his father's Sixties buildings. On the right, by Dingwall Avenue, is Electric House faced with Portland stone. This now listed building was completed just before the Second World War as the municipal electricity office. On the wall can be seen the words 'County Borough of Croydon Electricity Department'.

7. Continue over George Street into Park Lane to pass the huge Nestlé building on the corner of Park Street. The 260 foot high Sixties block replaced the Greyhound coaching inn. Almost opposite is the Fairfield Halls built in 1962 on the site of Fair Field where the annual fair was held from 1314 until the mid 19th century. The adjoining Ashcroft Theatre is named after Croydon born Dame Peggy Ashcroft. Beyond St George's Walk go right into Katharine Street to pass the town hall. The carved figure of Archbishop Whitgift can be seen to the right of the entrance and enthroned on the pavement is Queen Victoria. At the end go right along the High Street to the crossroads by the Whitgift Hospital.

8. The Whitgift Hospital was built as a home for 16 men and 16 women. When founded in 1596 by the Archbishop this was on the edge of the town with George Street at the side, then known as Pond Street. Go left down Crown Hill where there is a view of the parish church tower. At the bottom go left into Surrey Street to find the Dog and Bull.

⑮ Wallington
The Duke's Head

This walk starts at an attractive corner at the bottom of Wallington's hill and below some attractive cottages. Until the railway arrived on the open fields up the hill in 1847 this was just a hamlet near Beddington. Now the latter is just a manor house and church without its village. This route links the two by way of Beddington Park where the ornamental lake is fed by the infant River Wandle just as it once fed the manor's moat.

The Duke's Head on Wallington Green is in the oldest part of Wallington. Holy Trinity church, towering up at the back, was only built in 1867. The pub existed as a thatched cottage called Bowling Green House in 1726. Between 1740 and 1806 it was a lodging house which makes the recent addition of a hotel to the pub appropriate. A note in the 1857 property valuation reads: 'This is a pleasant and commodious rural Public House doing a remunerative business. It is let at £70 per year.'

The main entrance of this two bar pub is on the Green rather than the main road. Recent refurbishment has left the interior looking timeless with prints crowded on the walls, tankards hanging from the beams and even a warming pan on view. There is outdoor seating at the back as well as the front where people spill onto the green in the summer.

This has been a Young's house since 1857 although Young's beers have been available here since 1832 – the year of the Great Reform Bill. In the 1920s and 30s Young's bought some of the surrounding cottages to expand the pub. During the Second World War it was damaged by bombs but a notice on the stable wall at the back of the pub still reads 'Duke's Head Livery and bait stables' (bait was a term for the feeding of horses). It is a Grade II listed building.

There is good lunchtime food which might include a bacon and egg roll with salad and sweet and sour pork with salad. The pub is open all day. Telephone: 020 8647 1595.

- **HOW TO GET THERE:** The Duke's Head is on Wallington Green which is at the crossroads of the A232 Croydon Road and A237 Manor Road just east of Carshalton. The nearest station is Wallington. Turn left from the Railway Approach along Manor Road.
- **PARKING:** There is a pub car park for patrons.
- **LENGTH OF THE WALK:** 2$\frac{1}{2}$ miles. Map: OS Explorer 161 London South (GR 284647).

THE WALK

1. Walk across the Green to the traffic lights at the crossroads. Turn right along the main Croydon Road. Walk on the left side. After a very short distance the suburban houses make way for open space around Wallington Grammar School. When level with Bute Road (right) go beyond the footpath sign (left) and turn left into Beddington Park. The entrance is flanked by modern lodges.

2. Go ahead down an avenue. Just before the lake go right on another tree-lined path which curves eastward across the parkland. One or two trees have been felled but remain on the ground. There is a view to the left of the bridge carrying the carriage drive over the River Wandle. At a path junction turn right and follow the way towards the church. The path runs along the side of the walled burial ground.

3. At Church Road turn left to pass between the burial ground entrance and the church. This was once the centre of a village which gave its name to the Beddington Hundred of Surrey. The church (open Saturday mornings) has a Norman font and memorials to the Carew

family who lived next door at the manor from 1381 until 1859. The much rebuilt manor is now Carew Manor School but it incorporates a hall with a 15th-century hammerbeam roof. When first built the house was surrounded by a moat fed by the River Wandle. Henry VIII came here in 1531 to visit Sir Nicholas Carew eight years before his execution for his alleged part in a treason plot. Beyond Carew Manor School (right) go through the gateway to a junction by a lodge ahead. The half-timbered lodge was built in 1877 but to the right is a greater surprise – an early 18th-century dovecote.

4. The walk continues to the left of the lodge. Go past the gate and follow the way to find the River Wandle. Cross the bridge and keep forward on the park road (there may be some traffic). To the right is a cricket field. At the bend there is Parkside Café and a children's

Beddington church

playground. Behind is the site of a Roman bath. There is also evidence of Roman burials in the park. The path curves again to run alongside the park's northern boundary.

5. On approaching a gate turn left across the grass. (If the path is very muddy go ahead to the road and turn left to the lodge.) Follow the path just inside the park boundary. The way runs into trees. A footbridge carries the path over a ditch to a metalled path near the lodge (right). Turn left along the path which is the former carriageway to Carew Manor. Just before the bridge at the River Wandle turn right to follow the side of the lake. With the water to the left follow the waterside path which runs past topiary peacocks in the gardens of The Grange restaurant – a sympathetic 1967 replacement for the original house destroyed by fire. The path narrows and crosses a footbridge spanning a channel. At the far end cross the main waterfall and look right to see a view of Bridge House.

6. Bear right into the car park but before the road go left on to a path signed 'Carshalton Ponds' and part of the Wandle Trail. Go round the pond, crossing a footbridge, to Derek Avenue. Walk ahead along the residential road separated from the main road by another pond. At the far end continue forward on the main London Road. Ahead is the Rose and Crown. The road turns left to the crossroads at Wallington Green. Ahead is the Duke's Head.

16 Addington
Addington Village Inn

Addington village is separate from Addington housing estate, begun in 1934, but both are served by the new Tramlink. Old Addington preserves its pub, which is more flourishing than ever, a church and even a forge. The name Addington is probably most associated with Addington Palace which in the 19th century was the Archbishop of Canterbury's country home - Croydon Palace having been given up (see Walk 14). In the 20th century Addington Palace was home to the Royal School of Church Music which has now moved further south into Surrey. The palace and park have become a restaurant and golf course leaving the village little changed. The walk is across the borough boundary to a lonely church next to a Tudor mansion at West Wickham with the return route through ancient woodland.

Addington Village Inn is the Cricketers relaunched and so in the old part of the pub there are still plenty of cricket pictures on the wall including one of the village team whose club is one of the oldest in the country being founded before the MCC. But Addington is really famous for its palace and there are pictures of palace life in peace and war on the walls of the pub extension. Also featured are nearby Gravel Hill and West Wickham.

The pub is furnished with plenty of tables for those who want to enjoy a proper meal with the family but the atmosphere is still informal. There is even a rack of newspapers. In summer there is outdoor seating.

The menu is huge with baguettes, sandwiches and salads as well as Sunday roasts. There are several imaginative vegetarian dishes and a children's menu. The very popular desserts include an unusual chocolate fudge brownie with plenty of ice cream, bread and butter pudding and jam roly poly. This is a Bass house operating under the Innkeepers Fayre branding. It is open all day with food always available. Telephone: 01689 842057.

- **HOW TO GET THERE:** The Addington Village Inn is in Addington Village Road off the A2022 Kent Gate Way between Selsdon and Hayes. The nearest Tramlink stop is Addington. Cross the main road to the village.
- **PARKING:** There is a pub car park for patrons.
- **LENGTH OF THE WALK:** 3 miles. Map: OS Explorer 161 London South (GR 371639).

The Walk

1. Walk down to the village street from the new main door. Go right to pass the church where a large cross erected in 1911 in the churchyard records the Archbishops who lived at Addington Palace. The east end of the church is 12th-century but much restoration took place in the 19th century when the Archbishop was living nearby. The porch was added by Archbishop Howley in 1848. The reredos inside was added in 1896 as a memorial to Archbishop Benson who was the last to live here. Five archbishops are buried in the church. Continue along the street past Flint Cottage, built in 1796, and the end of Spout Hill.

2. The forge dates from at least 1740 and beyond are stables. The Wicket (left) is a residential road taking its name from the next door cricket ground, known as Cricket Meadow, where the village cricket club plays most summer Sundays. Later on the left there is the white Old Vicarage built in 1867.

3. At the end of the road turn onto the footpath signed as a cycleway to Bromley. There are woods to the left. Later the path is close to the main road (right). At the far end the path bends briefly into

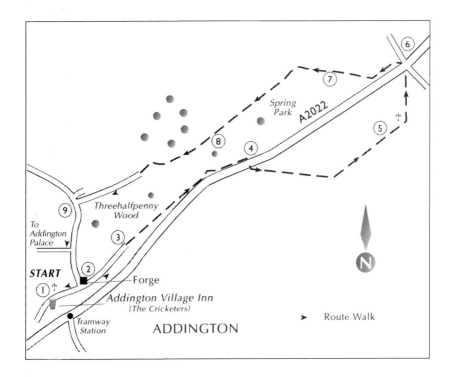

Threehalfpenny Wood before reaching a gate at the road by some buildings. This cluster of buildings is known as Kent Gate as the old Kent-Surrey boundary crosses the road by Gateway Lodge. This is now the boundary between the London Boroughs of Croydon and Bromley. Continue along the road – from Croydon into Bromley – past the buildings including Keeper's Cottage (left) and the entrance to Shirley Wanderers RFC. There is an expanse of grass belonging to Spring Park, where springs appear in winter, on the left.

4. Cross the road to the bus stop and go over the stile. The path is signposted 'Coneyhall'. At once bear half-left up the rising field and head towards the right of the college buildings ahead. The path soon levels out. There is a distant view of buildings and church towers in Hayes and Bickley just south of Bromley town centre. The path heads for the far corner of the field. Go over the stile on the left and walk ahead past a lonely tree on a path heading for the church. After a further stile the path is along a field boundary (right) and a line of poplar trees. Beyond a final stile the path rises up to a kissing gate at the churchyard. Steps take the path up to the church.

The path to West Wickham church

5. West Wickham Church has 14th-century arches but there may have been a Saxon church on this high vantage point. A Saxon manor here was replaced in 1480 with the present brick Wickham Court by Sir Henry Heydon who married Anne Boleyn, great aunt of Henry VIII's Queen of the same name. The Tudor mansion, now part of Sir John Rigby College, is an example of an early grand domestic house. Only go through the lychgate to see Wickham Court. The walk continues to the left on the churchyard path which drops down to a kissing gate by the memorial to members of the Beckenham Auxiliary Fire Service. This is now part of the London Loop route. Continue down the field to a second kissing gate by the road at a roundabout.

6. Cross over to the bottom of Corkscrew Hill. By the road sign go left into Sparrows Den playing field. Stay by the avenue on the left as far as the London Loop signpost. Here head half-right across the field to the corner of the wood.

7. Go past the seat and into the wood. Pass behind the Corporation of London sign to follow a winding path uphill through the trees. At the top bear left onto a path running alongside a wooden fence. Later the fence becomes see-through and then falls away leaving the high path to run ahead through the Spring Park woodland. Ignore all turnings but look out for a boundary stone on the left. This was placed here only in 1996 on the borough boundary which is also marked by an ancient ditch and bank. There are some small-leaved lime trees here.

8. Beyond the stone the path is in Threehalfpenny Wood. But soon the path bears gently round to the right to cross a firm bridleway. Ahead the path narrows to go under an arch of holly. Do not go ahead with the London Loop route but turn left on to the bridleway. Almost at once there is a fence to the right marking the garden of Hithe House. The way is metalled from its entrance. Follow this road to the end. Cross the road and turn left to walk down Spout Hill.

9. The pavement is raised above the road and soon passes the Lion Lodges, the village entrance to Addington Palace. The palace and its gateway date from the 1770s. At the bottom of the hill turn right to pass the church and reach Addington Village Inn.

⓱ Chislehurst
The Queen's Head

Chislehurst means 'wood on gravel' and much of the extensive Common is woodland. Countryside so close to central London, some owned by the National Trust, is a surprise as are the French royal associations. This walk links three unusual churches. The fine Annunciation in the High Street was built on the profits of Hymns Ancient & Modern, St Nicholas' is the medieval church and St Mary's has a chapel built for Napoleon III. A gentle summer walk ending late in the evening would not be out of place here for Chislehurst was home of the inventor of British Summer Time.

The 16th-century Queen's Head is the last house in the High Street before Prick End Pond and the Common. Outside is a cluster of footpath signs. The pub's recent renovation has given the interior a feeling of light, with pink walls and framed modern prints. The floor is bare boards around the bar but carpeted in the sitting areas where there are sofas and seats with cushions which help retain the homely atmosphere. Logs stacked by the fires add to the cosy feel in winter whilst some sheltered outside seating at the back is popular in summer.

The pub was once noted for its large ploughman's but now the bar menu is extensive and includes deep fried mushrooms, burgers and mixed grill as well as soup and sandwiches. The fish and chips come in a generous portion and there are always at least three vegetarian dishes. Food is served most of the day. This is a Bass house under the Ember Inn branding with Carling and Guinness available. It is open all day. Telephone: 020 829 2873.

- **HOW TO GET THERE:** The Queen's Head is at the south end of the A208 High Street at Chislehurst West. Buses 162 and 429 run from Chislehurst Station to the High Street.
- **PARKING:** There is a car park at the back of the pub for patrons.
- **LENGTH OF THE WALK:** 3 miles. Map: OS Explorer 162 Greenwich and Gravesend (GR 439708).

THE WALK

1. Turn left out of the pub forecourt to pass Prick End Pond. Bear right into Prince Imperial Road to pass the Methodist church completed in 1870 in Kentish Early English style. Where the houses end leave the pavement and take the bridlepath running ahead through the trees parallel to the road. On crossing the second road look left to see the memorial to Napoleon III's son the Prince Imperial who was killed in South Africa. After a short distance there is a glimpse through the trees to the right of Camden Place where the Imperial Family lived.

2. The main entrance to Camden Place, now a golf clubhouse, can be seen at the Hangman's Corner road junction ahead. Camden Place was the home of historian and writer William Camden in James I's reign. The present building dates from about 1717 and was built for the first Earl of Camden, the radical Lord Chancellor who in 1765 took his title from here. The London Borough of Camden is named after him because as landowner he granted leases for the erection of the first 1,400 houses which became Camden Town. In the early 19th century Camden Place was infamous following the murder in 1813 of Thomas Bonar and his wife by their manservant. Later in the century it was home to Nathaniel Strode who had connections with the French court and lent the house to the exiled Empress Eugènie. Her husband Napoleon III joined her here in 1870. Crowds would gather at the gate to watch the family drive out. Napoleon died at the house in 1873 and the Empress stayed on until 1881. Opposite, and marked with a blue plaque, is Cedars erected in 1893 by builder William Willett who

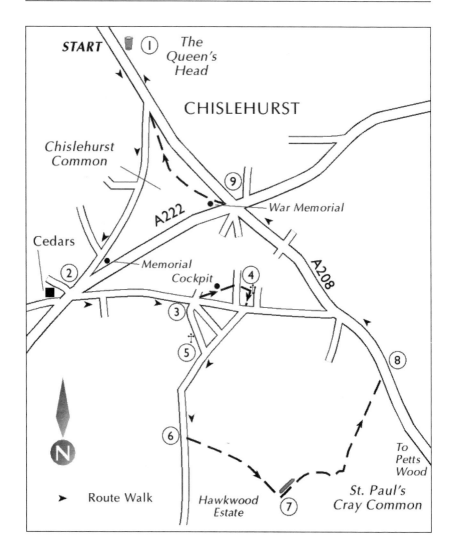

START ① The Queen's Head

CHISLEHURST

Chislehurst Common

Cedars

A222

— War Memorial

⑨

— Memorial Cockpit

②

④

③

⑤

⑥

⑧

Route Walk

Hawkwood Estate ⑦

To Petts Wood

St. Paul's Cray Common

A208

N

invented British Summer Time. He advocated daylight saving in 1908 and the Daylight Saving Bill was eventually passed in 1916, the year after his death. At this road junction go left across the end of Prince Imperial Road and Bromley Road to walk up Watts Lane alongside the cricket ground (right). Soon there is a view south (right) of countryside below.

3. On reaching the green bear half-left across the grass towards the church. To the left is a sunken area which is the rare remains of a cockpit – cockfighting was outlawed in 1834. The path joins a metalled path running towards the church. Go through the church gate. The porch entrance is round to the right.

4. St Nicholas' is the old parish church with the Scudbury Chapel containing the body of Sir Edmund Walsingham who was knighted by Henry VIII in 1513 after the defeat of the Scots at the Battle of Flodden Field. Leave the churchyard by the lychgate on the south side. Walk down Hawkwood Lane ahead.

5. Where Crown Lane joins there is St Mary's church. Here the Empress Eugènie attended mass. The chapel added to the south side was built by her for the body of her husband Napoleon but he now lies in Farnborough Abbey. However, there is a recumbent effigy of the Prince Imperial who is buried here. Continue down the lane which at a bend by the Old Laundry becomes Botany Bay Lane.

6. Where a footpath is signed to the left leave the lane and pass a National Trust sign at the entrance to the Hawkwood Estate. Keep to the right of the central fence. There is a view to the right over countryside between Orpington and Bromley. At the far end the path runs downhill through the end of Walk Wood to a pond.

7. Follow the boarded path round two sides of the pond. The path bends uphill round a field – there may be sheep here. At the top there is a Petts Wood National Trust sign and a view south to the wood. It was whilst riding in Petts Wood that Willett had his idea which led to the introduction of British Summer Time. Here turn left to a junction and go right to meet a T-junction at a bend. Turn left to follow the bridlepath through the wood on St Paul's Cray Common. Follow this path to a road. (But if the way is muddy take the parallel path which appears to the right beyond a four-way junction.)

8. At the road cross over to the pavement and turn left. At a bus stop cross back to a pavement on the left. Follow this main road past Manor Park Road (left) to the Bull's Head on the corner of Church Lane. This is the shopping centre of Chislehurst and beyond here the road becomes Royal Parade where a chemist was By Appointment to the Imperial Family. Opposite is the village sign showing Elizabeth I knighting Thomas Walsingham during her visit here in 1597. Continue to the crossroads by the war memorial.

9. Follow the path behind the war memorial which runs into the wood. At a junction turn right on to the main path towards the High Street. At the far end cross the entrance to Prince Imperial Road and go ahead to find the Queen's Head on the right beyond the pond.

18 Keston
The Fox

There is a red bus stop attached to the wall of the pub but this is the only evidence that this historic area is embraced by London. Here you will find the source of a river, ancient earthworks and a public footpath where a decision of world importance was taken. This is a short hilly walk in one of the best places in the London Borough of Bromley to see birds.

The Fox is a tall three-storey Victorian pub in the heart of Keston next to the post office and opposite the shops but with a green view to be enjoyed by those sitting outside in the summer. Darts and pool are played here and one wall has shelves full of much read books. It is a comfortable place and walkers will feel at home even after a muddy walk.

Food includes baked potatoes with tuna and sweetcorn topping and salad. Exotic sandwiches can be served with chips. This is a Whitbread Wayside house specialising in cask ales and Southwold bitter is on draught. The pub is open all day with food available at lunchtime and in the evenings. Telephone: 01689 852053.

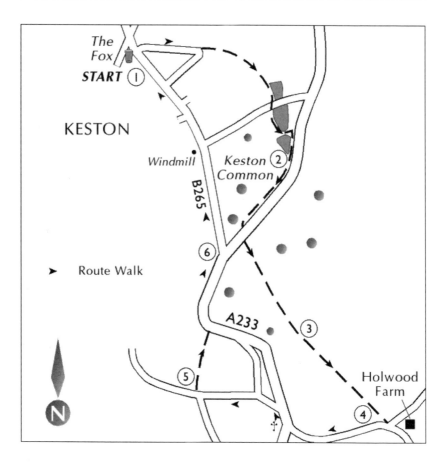

- **HOW TO GET THERE:** The Fox is at the northern entrance to Keston on the B265 south of Bromley. Bus 146 runs from Bromley South Station on Mondays to Saturdays.
- **PARKING:** There is a pub car park for patrons.
- **LENGTH OF THE WALK:** 3 miles. Map: OS Explorer 147 Sevenoaks and Tonbridge (GR 413645).

THE WALK

1. Cross the road to go down Lakes Road opposite the post office. This is part of the London Loop with waymarks. At the end go ahead on the metalled path alongside the horse ride. Soon the ride peels away as the path runs gently downhill into the wood. The way becomes rough and may ford a stream before rising. At the top of the slope the first of the

Wilberforce seat near Keston

Keston Ponds can be seen (left). Keep forward to a road. Cross over and pass a second pond but soon bear left to walk between ponds. Follow the edge of the third pond (right) to reach Caesar's Well where water bubbles up. This not only feeds the ponds but is also the source of the River Ravensbourne which eventually enters the River Thames as Deptford Creek.

2. Go ahead up steps to a car park. Here go half-left across the open space to a gateway at the start of a sunken path which runs parallel to the nearby road (left). The earthworks here may have originally been a cattle pound. Follow the way ahead and at a path junction turn left to the main road. Cross the road with care to take the path ahead. This runs in a straight line through woodland. At the highest point there is a seat with an older seat behind a railing.

3. This spot is part of the grounds of Holwood which was the home of William Pitt the Younger who became Prime Minister in 1783 at the age of 25. The stone seat was placed here by Earl Stanhope in 1869 to mark the spot where in 1788 William Wilberforce informed Pitt that he intended to abolish slavery. Later Wilberforce wrote: 'I well remember after a conversation with Mr Pitt in the open air at the root of an old oak tree at Holwood, just above the steep descent into the vale Keston, I resolved to give notice on a fit occasion in the House of Commons of my intention to bring forward the abolition of the slave trade.' The tree stump remains but a new oak, grown from an acorn taken from the historic oak, is behind the fence by the commemorative seat. Continue along the path which now drops downhill (do not go right on the wide path) to barriers. The path is fenced as it runs ahead between fields. Beyond more barriers there is a road junction by Holwood Farm.

4. Leave the London Loop to go right along Downe Road pavement. At the far end cross the main road and turn right. After a short distance go left into Church Road to find Keston church. There was a Saxon church on the site but the dedication remains unknown so this is still just 'Keston church'. Parts of the present building are Norman and the nave and chancel are about 1250. With a rising population the church was extended in 1878. The latest addition is the 1992 glassed-in cloister-style link to the new hall. Continue down the road passing Glebe House (left), Rectory Road (right) and Glebe Cottage (left).

5. At the junction with Jackass Lane (ahead) and Blackness Lane go right on a footpath. The way gently climbs the hill alongside a field where there are usually horses. Near the top the way becomes stepped. At the high road go left.

6. On approaching a junction, and before the bus stop, go left on a path running through woodland. Cross a car park to continue forward over grass to join a road. Follow the verge past the Flint Research Institute and the village hall. Next comes The Mill House and a black weatherboarded windmill on a brick base built in 1716. It stopped working in 1878 after a storm. Opposite is a war memorial and Fishponds Road. Keep ahead to the start of a pavement which should be followed through Keston to the Fox.

⑲ Downe
The Queen's Head

Downe, the most rural part of the London Borough of Bromley, is where Charles Darwin lived. The village is called Downe with an 'e' following confusion in the 19th century with County Down in Ireland. However, Darwin's house retained the old spelling and is still known as Down House. 'The charm of the place to me is that almost every field is intersected by one or more footpaths', wrote Darwin. 'I never saw so many walks in any other county. It is surprising to think London is only 16 miles off.' This walk follows the footpaths over land which was Darwin's outdoor laboratory and passes the front of his house on the way out of the village and the back on the return.

The Queen's Head is a Victorian pub in the High Street and next to the church. The name refers to Queen Elizabeth I who is depicted on the sign and visited the church for a christening in 1559. In summer patrons stand outside watching the planes from nearby Biggin Hill. In winter they enjoy the log fire inside. There is a children's room and in the back yard a surprise aviary.

The words 'Darwin Bar' appear in the glass on the doors. Inside there are small tables and often newspapers for those on their own to read. This is a free house with Burton Ale, Marston's Pedigree and Tetley's available. A wide range of food is served at lunchtime. The pub is open on weekdays from 11 am to 3 pm and 5.30 pm to 11 pm and all day at weekends. Telephone: 01689 852145.

- **HOW TO GET THERE:** The Queen's Head is in the High Street. Bus 146 runs from Bromley South Station on Mondays to Saturdays.
- **PARKING:** There is street parking.
- **LENGTH OF THE WALK:** $2^1/_2$ miles. Map: OS Explorer 147 Sevenoaks and Tonbridge (GR 433617).

THE WALK

1. Turn left out of the pub in the village square. The church dates from 1291 and has a modern window marking Robin Knox-Johnson's round the world voyage. In the chancel there is a plaque to John Lubbock, the first Lord Avebury, who invented bank holidays. He also circumnavigated the globe but ceased attending church when his friend Charles Darwin in the congregation was attacked from the pulpit by the vicar as 'The infidel and naturalist in our midst'. Now there is a Darwin memorial sundial on the tower. The big 1950 east window, showing the crucifixion, is by Evie Hone. Walk up Luxted Road.

2. After a short distance go left between the entrance to Trowmers and a willow tree. Bear left just before a house to follow a walled path leading to a field. Go ahead along the edge of the field and turn right at the corner. After a short distance go left through a gap to enter another field. Over to the left there is a farm. Turn right to follow the hedge to a kissing gate in the corner. Down House can be seen ahead. Bear slightly left across the field to a stile by the road.

Down House, opposite, is a late 18th-century farmhouse where naturalist Charles Darwin lived with his large family from 1842 until his death in 1882. Here he worked on his then controversial book *The Origin of Species* explaining his theory of evolution by natural selection. He also wrote many other books here including *The Descent of Man* exploring man's common ancestry with apes. Darwin's wife lived on here until 1896 and on her centenary in 1996 the house passed into the care of English Heritage. In the intervening century the house had been preserved by the British Association for the Advancement of Science, the Royal College of Surgeons and the

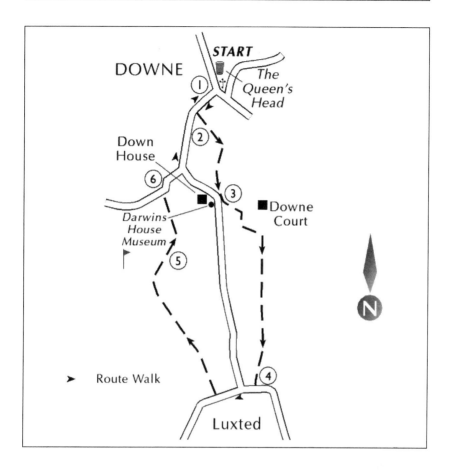

Natural History Museum. Darwin's chair and desk remain in the ground floor study. Also preserved are the hostile *Punch* cartoons he saved. Although the ground floor is much as Gladstone would have seen it during his visit in 1876, the upstairs is a museum with displays on Darwin's five year voyage sailing round the world aboard *The Beagle* shortly before moving here. Only cross the stile if wishing to visit Down House now (for opening times see below). The walk passes the garden entrance later.

3. Go past the stile (right) to the end of the field and turn left to follow the fence. The buildings ahead are Downe Court which in Elizabeth I's reign became home to a Venetian glass maker Giacomo Verzelini. He taught the English how to make crystal drinking glasses and is buried in Downe church. Go over the stile ahead and past the

Charles Darwin's Sandwalk

turning (right) to cross a stile on the right. Walk over the grass passing a black barn (left) to a further stile. Pass in front of Downe Court Farmhouse and across a farm road to a kissing gate. At once go left. At the field corner bear right and keep ahead. The way crosses a path junction. At the far end of the field go through a gap and continue ahead over open ground. Later there is a boundary to the right before the path reaches a field corner. Go over the wooden stile and follow a fenced path to a second stile. A narrow enclosed path leads to a road.

4. Turn right along the road to the hamlet of Luxted. Keep ahead down Birdhouse Lane by the post box at the side of Dunoon Cottages. Walk as far as the top of a hill. Here go right by Moonrakers, a typical Kent house. The path bends gently downhill. In summer the trees create a tunnel. At the end keep ahead along the side of a field and continue through a wood. Suddenly there is a view (left) of a golf course in a valley. Soon the path runs on to a corner of the golf course. Go forward but look out for a path running into the trees (right). Here, where orchids are to be found, turn right and go up a stepped path to a stile. Go forward before bearing half-left up the field passing a lonely tree (right).

5. Go over the stile in the corner. Here a gate on the right leads into the grounds of Down House. Beyond the gate there is Darwin's Sandwalk to the right and his kitchen garden to the left. The Sandwalk was Darwin's thinking path where the great scientist walked every morning in deep thought. In the walled kitchen garden, which is slowly being restored, he grew strawberries, 18 different kinds of potato, peas, beans, cabbage including open leaf cabbage, Brussels sprouts, 54 varieties of gooseberry, nuts and roses. Only to visit the house continue through the kitchen garden to find the visitors' entrance. The walk continues ahead from the stile and past the outside of the kitchen garden wall (right). Follow the narrow path to West Hill.

6. Turn right along the lane to the main road. Turn left past Downe Lodge. Walk on the right to face oncoming traffic until reaching the start of the pavement. Follow the road to the village centre and the Queen's Head.

ATTRACTION ON THE ROUTE
Down House and gardens (see above) are open from February to Christmas on Wednesday to Sunday, 10 am to 6 pm (winter 4 pm). Admission charge. The ticket includes an audio tour and there is a café. Telephone: 01689 859119.

20 Kenley
The Wattenden Arms

Kenley Common still has one of Croydon's once famous airports although now it is used mostly by air cadets and a glider club. In its early days the airfield saw the launch of a balloon from which suffragette leaflets were to be scattered over Parliament but the wind took it south to Caterham. Lloyd George flew from here to the Paris Peace Conference in 1919. In the Second World War the RAF was joined here by the Free French forces. There are fields and the occasional notice bearing the arms of the Corporation of London which protects this London countryside including Happy Valley. Also visited on this walk is Old Coulsdon which retains all the elements of a village.

The Wattenden Arms is on the southern edge of Kenley Common and has the feel of being deep in the countryside. Indeed, although within the London Borough of Croydon, it is not far from the Surrey border. So hidden is the 18th-century country pub that it has missed out on many a pub award although that does not worry all those who do know of its existence. It has recently been redecorated, but the walls still have

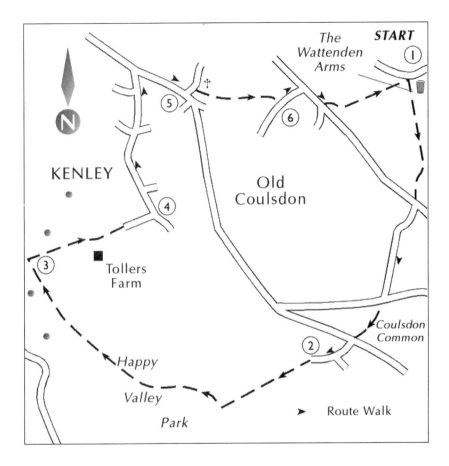

plenty of pictures from the days when many of the customers came from the nearby Kenley Aerodrome. A photograph shows the aftermath of just one of more than a hundred German attacks on the RAF base in the 1940s.

There is a single bar with food served at one end near the garden doors. The menu includes such dishes as cottage pie and breaded plaice and there are jacket potatoes with toppings as well as salads and sandwiches. This is a Bass house with London Pride and Worthington available. It is open all day. Telephone: 020 8763 9131.

● **HOW TO GET THERE:** The Wattenden Arms is at the south end of Old Lodge Lane which runs south from the A23 at Reedham just south-west of Purley.

- **PARKING:** In the pub's car park opposite.
- **LENGTH OF THE WALK:** 4 miles. Map: OS Explorer 146 Dorking, Box Hill and Reigate (GR 323582).

THE WALK

1. Turn left out of the pub and walk down the lane for a very short distance. When level with The Thatched Cottage go right through a gate and left. After a few yards go left through a gap and back to the lane. Cross with care to the stile at the beginning of the rough lane (leading to The Haven) opposite. A waymark indicates that this is part of the London Loop.

Go ahead up the field, cutting the corner as indicated by the usually worn path. Keep near the left hand boundary as the way gently bears round to the right to reach a stile by an observatory. Follow a metalled road and beyond a gate go half-right on a very narrow path through the trees. There is a Loop waymark. At a junction go right, but not sharp right, downhill through the trees. The steep path runs down to a road. Go ahead up Rydon's Lane which narrows as it climbs up onto Coulsdon Common. At a T-junction cross the road and go ahead across the Common. Soon there are cottages over to the left. Cross Coulsdon Road to go ahead up Fox Lane.

2. Keep on past the Fox pub and through a gateway. Here there is grass to the left. At the far end go ahead down the wooded path. Soon the way bears right into the open to give a view down Happy Valley. Continue ahead along the top side of the valley. Later the path runs downhill. Here go ahead to follow the path running along the valley floor. Meanwhile the London Loop now turns away to the left to run on the far side of the valley. The valley floor path soon runs through trees to become a wide grass way with woodland on both sides. Shortly after crossing a path junction the way comes to an end at a six-way junction.

3. Turn right up the path signposted 'Bridleway 742'. The path runs steeply up the side of the valley. Ignore all turnings and eventually the way is flat as it passes a house and Tollers Farm. Where the lane divides at Tollers Cottage keep left to a junction.

4. Turn left along residential Tollers Lane. Keep ahead at a crossroads and in a short distance there is the green at Old Coulsdon complete with a pond. At once turn right to reach the shops.

5. At the shops cross the road to the war memorial on the corner of Canon's Hill to reach the church beyond the lychgate with its stone stile. The church was built 1260 as a daughter church of Chertsey

Old Coulsden pond

Abbey. On the right of the altar are fine examples of a piscina and a sedilia – a basin and seats for the priest, deacon and sub-deacon at high mass. The flint tower is 15th-century. The surprise is the new church, joining on the south side, which was added in 1959 to serve the rising post war population. The new high altar has a dramatic but delicate baldachino. The walk continues down the side of The Corner Cottage by the church entrance. The enclosed path runs along the side of the churchyard, giving a view of the 'new' church, and along the bottom of several gardens. Where the way turns sharply right keep ahead downhill on the rough path to houses.

6. At a road go left down to a junction. Here turn right into Caterham Drive. Beyond a bus stop and opposite Keston Avenue turn left onto a footpath. The way rises steeply up a wooded hillside to a track. At the top go ahead to meet Old Lodge Lane. The Wattenden Arms is to the right. To avoid walking on the road go ahead up the steps to the field. Go right and right again at the white building. Opposite The Thatched Cottage turn left for the Wattenden Arms.